THE
POET'S CRAFT

A HANDBOOK OF
RHYME, METRE AND VERSE

SANDY BROWNJOHN

Hodder & Stoughton

A MEMBER OF THE HODDER HEADLINE GROUP

Acknowledgements:
The publishers would like to thank the following for their kind permission to reproduce copyright material:

Copyright Text:
piii *Mastering the Craft* by Vernon Scannell © Vernon Scannell, *Collected Poems 1950–1996*, Robson Books Ltd. Reproduced by kind permission of the author; p2 an extract from *Dunwich to Sizewell: Suffolk* by Sandy Brownjohn © Sandy Brownjohn, *Both Sides of the Catflap*, 1996. Reproduced by permission of Hodder and Stoughton Limited; p12 an extract from *Owl in the Afternoon* by Sandy Brownjohn © Sandy Brownjohn, *Both Sides of the Catflap*, 1996. Reproduced by permission of Hodder and Stoughton Limited; p55 two haiku from 'A Norfolk Bestiary' by Sandy Brownjohn © Sandy Brownjohn, *Both Sides of the Catflap*; p57 *Kyrielle* by Sandy Brownjohn © Sandy Brownjohn, *In and Out of the Shadows*, Oxford University Press Children's Books, 2000; p60 *The Semantic Limerick According to the Shorter Oxford English Dictionary (1933)* by Gavin Ewart © Gavin Ewart. Reproduced by kind permission of Margo Ewart; p61 two ruthless rhymes by Harry Graham, *Ruthless Rhymes*, Edward Arnold, 1994; p78 *Ice* by Kevin Crossley-Holland © Kevin Crossley-Holland, *The Exeter Book Riddles*, Penguin Books, 1979, Revised edition 1993; p87 *Have a Good Time* by W. H. Auden, *Collected Shorter Poems 1927–1957*, 1996. Reproduced by kind permission of Faber and Faber Ltd.

Every effort has been made to trace copyright holders of material reproduced in this book. Any rights not acknowledged will be acknowledged in subsequent printings if notice is given to the publisher.

Orders: please contact Bookpoint Ltd, 130 Milton Park, Abingdon, Oxon OX14 4SB. Telephone: (44) 01235 827720, Fax: (44) 01235 400454. Lines are open from 9.00–6.00, Monday to Saturday, with a 24 hour message answering service. Email address: orders@bookpoint.co.uk

British Library Cataloguing in Publication Data

A catalogue record for this title is available from The British Library

ISBN 0 340 80292 8

First published 2002

Impression number   10 9 8 7 6 5 4 3 2 1

Year   2008 2007 2006 2005 2004 2003 2002

Copyright © 2002 Sandy Brownjohn

Typeset by Fakenham Photosetting Limited, Fakenham, Norfolk

Printed in Great Britain for Hodder & Stoughton Educational, a division of Hodder Headline Plc, 338 Euston Road, London NW1 3BH by The Bath Press, Bath.

Mastering The Craft

To make the big time you must learn
The basic moves: left jab and hook,
The fast one-two, right-cross; the block
And counter-punch; the way to turn
Opponents on the ropes; the feint
To head or body; uppercut;
To move inside the swing and set
Your man up for the kill. But don't
Think that this is all; a mere
Beginning only. It is through
Fighting often you will grow
Accomplished in manoeuvres more
Subtle than the text books know:
How to change your style to meet
The unexpected move that might
Leave you open to the blow
That puts the lights out for the night.

The same with poets: they must train,
Practise metre's footwork, learn
The old iambic left and right,
To change the pace and how to hold
The big punch till the proper time,
Jab away with accurate rhyme;
Adapt the style or be knocked cold.
But first the groundwork must be done.
Those poets who have never learnt
The first moves of the game, they can't
Hope to win.   Yet here comes one,
No style at all, untrained and fat,
Who still contrives to knock you flat.

Vernon Scannell

CONTENTS

Verse

(Entries marked with a star * are specific forms as opposed to more general poetic terms and devices.)

Introduction

This handbook is intended for anyone who has an interest in the craft of poetry – both amateur and professional writers, as well as students and teachers of English. It does not aspire to being the definitive reference book on prosody as that, of necessity, would have to be a much longer affair.

When I first became interested in writing poetry I, like many people, knew very little about its composition. I poured out a kind of sub-standard free verse, rambling, full of clichés, and ultimately unsatisfactory. Then, like a number of other writers, I discovered *The Poet's Manual and Rhyming Dictionary* by Frances Stillman which introduced me to the different forms and techniques in poetry. It was a liberation. I enjoyed trying out new forms and rhyme schemes. Far from being restricting, this self-imposed apprenticeship approach began to educate my ear and to provide challenges that were exciting to try to meet. This practical way of learning by doing taught me more about poetry than any study course could hope to provide. It not only made me more interested in the craft – and thereby more appreciative of what poets do – but also took me back to reading the poetry of earlier centuries, much of which had seemed dull and remote at school. I owe a great debt to Frances Stillman.

In recent years there have been a number of good books on the practice of poetry, most written by writers, so why the need for another one? Well, what I found I wanted for everyday use was a simple and easy reference book in which I could find at a glance what I needed to know about any form, metre or rhyme scheme. I wanted a dictionary of sorts, and this is what *The Poet's Craft* offers.

The book is in three sections – Rhyme, Metre and Verse – and each is arranged alphabetically, with a clear description and examples for every entry. At the beginning is a list of contents for each section so people can see if a term is in the book and where it can be found. I have included a number of little-used forms for interest, although this is by no means a comprehensive list.

I hope *The Poet's Craft* will encourage others to explore this greatest of literary arts, but at the very least be a useful reference book – for who but the most retentive of minds can remember the order of the repeated words in a sestina?

Sandy Brownjohn

Rhyme

From *Words*

Out of us all
That make rhymes,
Will you choose
Sometimes –
As the winds use
A crack in the wall
Or a drain,
Their joy or their pain
To whistle through –
Choose me,
You English words?
. . .

Let me sometimes dance
With you,
Or climb,
Or stand perchance
In ecstasy,
Fixed and free
In a rhyme,
As poets do.

Edward Thomas

ALLITERATION
Alliteration is a sequence of repeated initial sounds before stressed syllables. In practice, this is usually the same sound at the *beginnings* of words (not necessarily the same letters). Alliteration is a form of **rhyme**.*

Examples:

1. From *The Tempest* by Shakespeare
Full **f**athom **f**ive thy **f**ather lies

2. From *Spring* by Gerard Manley Hopkins
Nothing is as beautiful as Spring –
When **w**eeds, in **w**heels, shoot **l**ong and **l**ovely and **l**ush;

3. From *The Eagle* by Alfred, Lord Tennyson
He **cl**asps the **cr**ag with **cr**ooked hands;
Close to the sun in **l**onely **l**ands

AMPHISBÆNIC RHYME
(pronounced AM-fis-BEE-nik) This is a very rare rhyming device which takes its name from the mythical monster, the amphisbæna, which had a head at each end of its body. In the same way, it is as if a word turns round on itself to create its **rhyme**, as the following examples show: *bard* and *drab; regal* and *lager; wolf* and *flow; sloop* and *pools.*

Example:

In life, each man is given his remit –	a
At birth an unseen hand will set the timer –	a
Then he must choose his path, for good or evil,	b
And do his best to cheat the clock and live.	b

SB (Sandy Brownjohn)

ANAGRAM RHYME
This is another rare rhyming device. The **rhymes** are anagrams of themselves, i.e. the letters of one word are rearranged to create another word which is then used as the rhyme, as in *horse* and *shore; reactor* and *creator.*

Example:

From *Dunwich to Sizewell: Suffolk* by SB
Along this coast she rides her horse,

* Words which appear in bold are a cross reference to another entry within the book.

Pounding a wide and windswept shore,
Her foaming hair like shaggy tinsel
In the stormlight. Over inlets
Streams her flowing mane –
And no one speaks her name.

ASSONANCE (pronounced ASS-o-nance) Assonance is the
repetition of the same, or similar, vowel sounds in words very close
to each other so that the ear picks up the rhyming echoes. It is a
form of **rhyme** which is sometimes known as vocalic rhyme.

Examples:

1. From *Dover Beach* by Matthew Arnold

But now I only hear
Its melancholy, long, withdrawing roar,
Retreating, to the breath
Of the night-wind, down the vast edges drear
And naked shingles of the world.

2. From *Song of the Lotos-Eaters* by Alfred, Lord Tennyson

Music that brings *sweet sleep* down from the blissful skies.
Here are cool mosses *deep,*
And through the moss the ivies *creep,*
And in the *stream* the long-*leaved* flowers *weep,*
And from the craggy ledge the poppy hangs in *sleep.*

BEGINNING RHYME Beginning **rhyme** is the term applied to
verse where rhymes occur at the beginnings rather than the ends of
lines. It is a rarely used device.

Examples:

1. From *The Bridge of Sighs* by Thomas Hood

Mad from life's history,
Glad to death's mystery,
   Swift to be hurl'd –
Anywhere, anywhere
   Out of the world!

2. From *The Wreck of the Deutschland* by Gerard Manley Hopkins

Not out of his bliss

> *Springs* the stress felt
> Nor first from heaven (and few know this)
> *Swings* the stroke dealt –

CONSONANCE (pronounced CON-so-nance) Consonance is the repetition of the same, or similar consonant sounds. The vowel sounds will differ. The resulting effect may be of partial **rhyme** (also known as **half-rhyme**, near, imperfect, para or part-rhyme). It can also constitute **alliteration** with repeated initial sounds.

Example:

From *Miners* by Wilfred Owen

I thought of some who worked dark **pits**
Of war, and **died**
Digging the rock where Death re**putes**
Peace lies in**deed**.

Comforted years will sit soft-**chaired**
In rooms of **amber**;
The years will stretch their hands, well-**cheered**
By our lives' **ember**.

The centuries will burn rich **loads**
With which we **groaned**,
Whose warmth shall lull their dreaming **lids**,
While songs are **crooned**.
But they will not dream of us poor **lads**,
Lost in the **ground**.

Some poets prefer to see consonance as only the repetition of the final consonant sounds.

Example:

I Took my Power in my Hand by Emily Dickinson

I took my power in my hand
And went against the wor**ld**;
'Twas not so much as David had
But I was twice as bo**ld**.

I aimed my pebble, but myself
Was all the one that fe**ll** –

Was it Goliah was too large
Or was myself too small?

Consonance can also be used within lines to create an effect on the ear. This form of half-rhyme can add a musical texture to the sound of a poem which may, or may not, also be an example of **onomatopoeia.**

In the following nursery rhyme *Hickory dickory, dock*, the words, *clock* and *struck* are examples of consonance which are also onomatopoeic in that they echo the tick-tocking sound of the clock; and *one* is a half-rhyme for *down.*

Example:

Hickory, dickory, dock,
The mouse ran up the clock.
The clock struck one
The mouse ran down,
Hickory, dickory, dock.

DISSONANCE
Dissonance is the repetition or arrangement of sounds or rhythms which are harsh on the ear, in order to create an effect arising from the sense of the poem, such as reproducing discordant sound or suggesting unease. When read aloud lines and phrases containing dissonance are jarring rather than harmonious. Harder consonants, such as 'b', 'd', 'g', 'j', 'k', 'q', 'v', 'x' and 'z', and the harsher short vowels, such as in *jagged, clock,* and *bucket*, will help to achieve these effects. Sudden alterations in the rhythm of lines will also disconcert the ear.

(see also **assonance** and **consonance**)

In the following short extract from Alfred, Lord Tennyson's poem, *Morte D'Arthur*, King Arthur is very close to his death. After twice failing to obey the king's orders to throw the sword Excalibur into the lake, Sir Bedivere finally does as he had been ordered. Then, he carries the dying Arthur to the edge of the lake. The dissonance created by the words describe the clattering sound made by his feet and armour but also suggest the wild state of his mind and conscience, and the terrible, impending death of the once great king.

Example:

From *Morte D'Arthur* by Alfred, Lord Tennyson
His own thought drove him like a goad.
Dry clash'd his harness in the icy caves
And barren chasms, and all to left and right
The bare black cliff clang'd round him, as he based
His feet on juts of slippery crag that rang
Sharp-smitten with the dint of armed heels –
And on a sudden, lo! the level lake,
And the long glories of the winter moon.

END-RHYME
End-**rhyme** is simply a term applied to verse in which the rhymes occur at the ends of lines. This is the most common method of rhyming and is often the only kind of rhyme of which non-poets are aware.

Example:

On the Meetings of the Scotch Covenanters Anon
Informer, art thou in the tree,
Take heed lest there thou hangèd be;
Look likewise to thy foothold well
Lest, if thou slip, thou fall to hell.

EYE RHYME
(also known as spelling rhyme) An eye **rhyme** is one which looks as if it is an exact rhyme, by its spelling, but is actually pronounced differently.

Examples of such words are: *love, move* and *grove*; *bead* and *dead*; and of course, the various *ough* sounds, such as *tough, through, although, bough, cough* etc. Eye rhymes would be considered **half-rhyme**s.

Example:

The last four lines of this poem by Robert Herrick use eye rhymes.

To Dianeme by Robert Herrick
Sweet, be not proud of those two eyes
Which starlike sparkle in their skies;
Nor be you proud that you can see
All hearts your captives, yours yet free;

Be you not proud of that rich hair
Which wantons with the love-sick air;
Whenas that ruby which you **wear**,
Sunk from the tip of your soft **ear**,
Will last to be a precious **stone**
When all your world of beauty's **gone**.

FULL RHYME (also called **true rhyme** or **perfect rhyme**) Full **rhyme** is the term applied to words whose vowel and end-consonant sounds produce the exact same sound effect, while the beginning consonants are different. In other words, when spoken aloud the words sound exactly the same except for their beginnings. The following are examples of full rhymes:

● one syllable words: *cat, sat* and *mat; home, foam* and *comb;*

● two syllable words: *mother* and *brother; wearing* and *staring;*

● three syllable words: *remonstrate* and *demonstrate; Melanie* and *felony.*

Words such as *depu_ty_, hones_ty_, seven_ty_* and *dign_ity_,* or *car_diac_* and *zo_diac_,* can be said to rhyme, through the sounds of their final stressed syllables. However, they would not qualify to be called full, perfect or true because the preceding parts of the words do not have the same sound.

HALF-RHYME (also called near, part, imperfect, slant, or para-rhyme)

Half-**rhyme** is exactly what its name would suggest – two words which do not fully rhyme (as *cat* and *mat* <u>do</u>). However, half-rhymes do echo part of the sound of each other. For example, half-rhymes for *cat* might be *cut* or *cot, get* or *got,* or even *cap* or *stack.* Half-rhymes may be used at the ends of lines, or within the body of a poem where they can be very effective, setting up echoes of sound which can help to play on the senses and make the poem more memorable.

There are many different types of half-rhyme and many opinions on what does and what does not constitute half-rhyme. Some people will insist it is only the end-consonants that must be the same (see **consonance**). Some will say that it is permissible to have only the vowels the same, and that all vowels are interchangeable in their sound effects (see **assonance**). While others will accept words that rhyme only on their stressed syllables, such as _minder_ and _defined_, _ground_ and _profoundly_, _perusal_ and _inclusion_. Half-rhymes may also occur when words rhyme only on their unstressed syllables, such as _eventual_ and _factual_, _singing_ and _dancing_, _readable_ and _affordable_, _ridiculous_ and _bibulous_.

Some writers maintain that a poem should not mix **full rhyme**s with half-rhymes at the ends of lines, that they should use either one or the other throughout the whole poem. It must also be said that too often evidence of half-rhymes is merely evidence that a writer has been lazy or incompetent.

As to any rules governing the use of half-rhyme, a writer should listen to the effects and to the music of the poem. Think and hear what will work and if half-rhyme is used it should be a conscious decision, not the result of avoiding the hard work of finding a full rhyme or having to rephrase a line.

The possibilities

● The same end-consonant sounds, e.g. _drift_ and _bereft_, _lost_ and _mast_, _single_ and _angle_.

● The same vowel sounds, e.g. _start_ and _park_, _fame_ and _again_, _over_ and _sofa_.
  If one uses this form of half-rhyme there are certain rules about which consonants such words can end with (although writers may not want to stick to them). The following consonants in the table opposite belong together in groups and should either be used with another from their group, or with their opposite unvoiced sounds.

	Voiced Groups			Unvoiced Groups		
1	d	g	b	t	k	p
2	z	zh		s	sh	
3	v	th (as in **the**)		f	th (as in **th**umb)	
4	l	m	n	r		

● Different vowel sounds within the same basic structure of word (para-rhyme), e.g. *mutter* and *matter, story* and *starry, hopeless* and *hapless.*

● Stressed syllables only rhyming, e.g. *around* and *astounded, icy* and *device, believer* and *deceiving.*

● Unstressed syllables only rhyming, e.g. *floating* and *sinking, station* and *fiction, village* and *courage.*

● A stressed syllable rhyming with an unstressed syllable, e.g. *fur* and *slipper, go* and *fellow, ship* and *Philip.*

One writer who experimented with half-rhyme in the nineteenth century was the American poet, Emily Dickinson. The following is taken from one of her best-known poems.

The words *clock, tick* and *bark* are half-rhymes (also *look*, in the first line, is an example of **internal rhyme**), as are *tell* and *will* (and *walls* as an internal rhyme).

Example:

From *I Know Some Lonely Houses off the Road* by Emily Dickinson
How orderly the kitchen'd look by night,
With just a clock,
But they could gag the tick,
And mice won't bark;
And so the walls don't tell,
None will.

(see also **assonance, consonance,** and **rhyme**)

. . . .

IDENTICAL RHYME Identical **rhyme** is the term given to two
different, but related, rhyming techniques.

1. The repetition of the same word to make a rhyme. For example, most of the limericks written by Edward Lear finish with the same word as that used at the end of the first line.

Example:

> There was an Old Person of Cromer,
> Who stood on one leg to read Homer;
> When he found he grew stiff,
> He jumped over the cliff,
> Which concluded that Person of Cromer.

2. The use of a rhyming word which <u>sounds</u> the same, but is spelt differently and has a different meaning (these are known as homophones); e.g. *main* and *mane*; *bear* and *bare*; *rite, write* and *right*.

Neither of these forms of rhyme is really to be recommended, unless a writer wishes to create a particular effect. Poems should work on the ear as well as the eye, and listeners cannot be expected to visualise a different spelling of what they are hearing. Repetition of the same word, or even the same whole line, can, however, be very effective in the right situation, as the last stanza of the following poem famously shows.

Example:

> **From *Stopping by Woods on a Snowy Evening* by Robert Frost**
> The woods are lovely, dark and deep,
> But I have promises to keep,
> And miles to go before I sleep,
> And miles to go before I sleep.

Identical rhyme can also work well in humorous **light verse**, as the following example shows.

> Mary had a little lamb
> She also had a bear;
> I've often seen her little lamb,
> But never seen her bear.   (bare!)

. . . .

INTERNAL RHYME Internal **rhyme** is the term applied to
rhyming words which occur within the body of a poem rather than

at the ends of lines. There are different ways this can be achieved so that the ear hears the music of the rhyme.

1. Leonine rhyme has one word at the natural mid-point of a line, rhyming with one at the end of the same line. This sort of rhyme has figured prominently in old ballads and songs, as well as in magic spells, e.g. the opening incantatory line of the three witches in Shakespeare's *Macbeth:* 'Double, double, toil and trouble. . . .'

The following example contains some more famous witches.

Example:

From *The Masque of Queens* by Ben Jonson.

The Owl is *abroad*, the bat and the *toad*,
And so is the cat-a-mountain;
The ant and the *mole* both sit in a *hole*,
And frog peeps out o' the fountain.
The dogs they do *bay*, and the timbrels *play*,
The spindle is now a-turning;
The moon it is *red*, and the stars are *fled*,
But all the sky is a-burning:
The ditch is *made*, and our nails the *spade*:
With pictures *full*, of wax and *wool*,
Their livers I *stick* with needles *quick*;
There lacks but the *blood* to make up the *flood*.

And the opening of an old ballad:

Some years of *late*, in eighty-*eight*
    As I do well remember,
It was, some *say*, the tenth of *May*,
    And, some say, in September,
    And, some say, in September.

The Spanish *train* launch'd forth *amain*,
    With many a fine bravado,
Their (as they *thought*, but it proved *not*)
    Invincible Armado,
    Invincible Armado.

2. Two or more words rhyming within the same line.

a) **Full rhyme**
From *God's Grandeur* by Gerard Manley Hopkins
Generations have trod, have trod, have trod;
And all is *seared* with trade; *bleared, smeared* with toil;
And *wears* man's smudge and *shares* man's smell: the soil
Is bare now, nor can foot feel, being shod.

b) **Half-rhyme**
From *The Photograph* by Thomas Hardy
Then I vented a cry of *hurt*, and *averted* my eyes;
The spectacle was one that I could not bear,
To my deep and sad surprise;

From *Inversnaid* by Gerard Manley Hopkins
This darksome *burn*, horseback *brown*,
His rollrock highroad roaring down,
In *coop* and in *comb* the fleece of his *foam*
Flutes and *low* to the lake falls *home*.

3. Two, or more, words rhyming (either **full** or **half-rhyme**) in
adjacent lines.

From *Hope* by Emily Brontë
Hope was but a timid friend;
She sat without the *grated* den,
Watching how my *fate* would tend,
Even as selfish-hearted men.

From *Owl in the Afternoon* by SB
On *silent* wings from nowhere came the owl;
How *violent*, yet how soft, the *rush* of air
That *brushed* my hair.

PERFECT RHYME (see **full rhyme**)

ONOMATOPOEIA
Onomatopoeia is a figure of speech in which words imitate or echo the sound of what is being described. The sound of the words, or certain letters within them, work on the ear to reinforce the meaning of a poem.

For example, 's' and 'sh' sounds can naturally conjure up the sound of the sea, as in words such as o<u>ce</u>an, <u>sh</u>ell<u>s</u>, spla<u>sh</u>, <u>s</u>wi<u>sh</u>, <u>s</u>urf and wave-wa<u>sh</u>ed. Similarly, sharper sounds, such as 'k', 't', 'g', 'd' and 'b', can reproduce the effect of machines, engines or mechanical devices. An obvious example is the nursery rhyme, *Hi<u>ck</u>ory, di<u>ck</u>ory, do<u>ck</u>*, where the the harsh 'ck' sound is combined with the rhythm to suggest the ticking of the clock.

(see also **assonance, consonance** and **dissonance**)

Examples:

1. From *Come down, O Maid* by Alfred, Lord Tennyson
The moan of doves in immemorial elms,
And murmuring of innumerable bees.

2. From *Enoch Arden's Island* by Alfred, Lord Tennyson
The myriad shriek of wheeling ocean-fowl,
The league-long roller thundering on the reef,

In the following poem, the soft 'l', 's', 'f' and 'ing' sounds conjure up the idea of the falling snow.

3. From *London Snow* by Robert Bridges
When men were all asleep the snow came flying,
In large white flakes falling on the city brown,
Stealthily and perpetually settling and loosely lying,
⠀⠀⠀Hushing the latest traffic of the drowsy town;
Deadening, muffling, stifling its murmurs failing;
Lazily and incessantly floating down and down:
⠀⠀⠀Silently sifting and veiling road, roof and railing;
Hiding difference, making unevenness even,
Into angles and crevices softly drifting and sailing.

REPETITION There are many kinds of repetition used in poetry, but basically the term speaks for itself – it means that certain words or sounds are repeated in order either to emphasise something, to create an effect of sound or meaning, or as part of the form (e.g. **refrain**), to add a unifying and memorable aspect to the poem. Single sounds, whole words, phrases or lines can all be repeated. Repetition is a rhyming technique as the ear picks up the echo of sound, albeit the exact same echo. Repetition should always, however, be intended by the writer as part of the effect he or she wishes to create. Two well-known examples in twentieth century verse are *Silver* by Walter de la Mare, and *The Jolly Hunter* by Charles Causley, where the word *jolly* is repeated throughout the poem with a slightly different nuance of meaning each time and to great comic effect.

(see also **assonance, consonance, dissonance** and **identical rhyme**)

There are many examples of repetition at work in poetry. The following poems are a small selection.

Examples:

1. *NO!* by Thomas Hood

No sun – no moon!
No morn – no noon –
No dawn – no dusk – no proper time of day –
No sky – no earthly view –
No distance looking blue –
No road – no street – no 't'other side the way' –
No end to any Row –
No indications where the Crescents go –
No top to any steeple –
No recognitions of familiar people –
No courtesies for showing 'em –
No knowing 'em! –
No travelling at all – no locomotion,
No inkling of the way – no notion –
'No go' – by land or ocean –
No mail – no post –
No news from any foreign coast –
No Park – no Ring – no afternoon gentility –
No company – no nobility –
No warmth, no cheerfulness, no healthful ease,
No comfortable feel in any member –
No shade, no shine, no butterflies, no bees,
No fruits, no flowers, no leaves, no birds –
November!

2. From *Remember* by Christina Rossetti

Remember me when I am **gone away**,
   Gone far **away** into the silent land;
   When you can no more hold me by the hand,
Nor I half turn to go yet turning stay.
Remember me when no more day by day
   You tell me of your future that you planned:
   Only **remember me**; you understand
It will be late to counsel then or pray.

3. *Four Ducks on a Pond* by William Allingham

Four ducks on a pond,
A grass-bank beyond,
A blue sky of spring,
White clouds on the wing;
What a little thing
To remember for years –
To remember with tears!

4. From *The Charge of the Light Brigade* by Alfred, Lord Tennyson

'Forward, the Light Brigade!'
Was there a man dismay'd?
Not tho' the soldier knew
   Some one had blunder'd:
Theirs not to make reply,
Theirs not to reason why,
Theirs but to do and die:
Into the valley of Death
   Rode the six hundred.

Cannon to right of them,
Cannon to left of them,
Cannon in front of them
   Volley'd and thunder'd;
Storm'd at with shot and shell,
Boldly they rode and well,
   Into the jaws of Death,
   Into the mouth of Hell
     Rode the six hundred.

RHYME
Rhyme is the repetition of same or similar sounds so that they chime on the ear. Poetry was originally an oral art and is very akin to music. Rhyme might be compared to harmony in music – the repetition of similar sounds in words and letters being like the combination of harmonious notes which can create a memorable and attractive effect on a listener. There are many different ways of using rhyme in poetry, although the general public tends to be aware of only **full rhyme** (or near-full rhyme, such as *zodiac* and *cardiac*) which is expected to occur at the ends of lines. This whole section deals with the various different devices that can be used to create rhyming effects. A study of the terms will show that rhyme is infinitely more versatile than most people think.

TRUE RHYME (see **full rhyme**)

METRE

Metrical Feet

／　∪　／　∪　／　∪　／
Trochee trips from long to short.

∪　／　∪　／　∪　／　∪　／
From long to long in solemn sort

／　／　／　／　／　／　／　／∪
Slow **Spondee** stalks; strong foot yet ill able

／∪∪　／　∪　∪　／　∪　∪／∪∪
Ever to come up with **Dactyl** trisyllable.

∪／　∪　／　∪　／　∪　／
Iambics march from short to long.

∪　∪　／　∪∪　／　∪　∪　／∪　∪　／
With a leap and a bound the swift **Anapæsts** throng.

Samuel Taylor Coleridge

ALEXANDRINE

ALEXANDRINE In English verse an alexandrine is a line of 12 syllables written in **iambic** rhythm – an iambic **hexameter**. It is not often used as the hexameter is just that bit too long for English ears and the **pentameter** fits more easily into English speech rhythms. (As with other regular metres, poets will occasionally deviate from the strictly iambic **foot**.)

Example:

From *The Prisoner* by Emily Brontë

'Still let my tyrants know, I am not doomed to wear
Year after year in gloom, and desolate despair;
A messenger of Hope comes every night to me,
And offers for short life, eternal liberty.

He comes with western winds, with evening's wandering airs,
With that clear dusk of heaven that brings the thickest stars,
Winds take a pensive tone, and stars a tender fire,
And visions rise, and change, that kill me with desire.'

In French verse the alexandrine is a line of 12 syllables, usually containing four accents or beats.

(see also **metre**)

AMPHIBRACH

AMPHIBRACH An amphibrach (pronounced AM-fi-BRAK) is a metrical **foot** of three syllables – short, long, short (di-dum-di). The stress comes on the middle syllable, as in the words de*scend*ed, un*want*ed, Je*mim*a and ad*vant*age. Verse written predominantly in this **metre** would be called amphibrachic. It is not a metre particularly suited to English verse, though it does occur occasionally.

Examples:

1. From *How They Brought the Good News from Ghent to Aix* by Robert Browning

˘ ⁄ ˘|˘ ⁄ ˘ | ˘ ⁄ ˘| ˘ ⁄
I *sprang* to the *stir*rup, and *Jo*ris, and he;
I *gal*loped, I Dirck *gal*loped, I we *gal*loped I all three . . .

2. Nursery rhyme

To *mar*ket, I to *mar*ket, I to *buy* a I fat pig . . .

(see also **metre**)

ANAPÆST (pronounced AN-a-peest) An anapæst is a metrical foot of three syllables – short, short, long (di-di-dum). The stress comes on the final syllable. Verse written predominantly in this metre would be called anapæstic.

Examples:

```
ᴗ ᴗ  ⁄ | ᴗ ᴗ  ⁄  | ᴗ ᴗ ⁄ | ᴗ ᴗ  ⁄
```
1. I'm a shrimp, I'm a shrimp, and I live in the sea . . .

2. From *The Destruction of Sennacherib* by Lord Byron

The Assy | rian came down | like the wolf | on the fold,
And his co | horts were gleam | ing in pur | ple and gold;
And the sheen | on their spears | was like stars | on the sea,
When the blue | wave rolls night | ly on deep | Galilee.

(see also **metre**)

. . . .

BLANK VERSE Blank verse is the term given to non-rhyming lines of poetry written in **iambic pentameter** (di dum-di dum-di dum-di dum-di dum or ᴗ ⁄ – ᴗ ⁄ – ᴗ ⁄ – ᴗ ⁄ – ᴗ ⁄). It is said to represent the closest in rhythm to the normal speech patterns of the English language. Most people will be familiar with blank verse from reading or seeing Shakespeare's plays. It was the standard verse form for Elizabethan drama and was also used by Milton in his work, *Paradise Lost*. It has proved to be the most used **metre** for poets writing in English. Although, strictly speaking, there should be only ten syllables, blank verse allows for a more flexible approach. There will often be anything from 9 to 12 syllables, and sometimes the metre deviates from the iambic in places. However, the predominant rhythm is the five-stress line of the iambic pentameter.

Example:

Romeo and Juliet, Act 2, Scene 2 by William Shakespeare

But, soft! What light through yonder window breaks?
It is the east, and Juliet is the sun.
Arise, fair sun, and kill the envious moon,
Who is already sick and pale with grief
That thou her maid art far more fair than she.

. . . .

CÆSURA

CÆSURA A cæsura is a natural pause or break in a line of verse. (Its **scansion** is usually denoted by a double line: ‖.) A cæsura may be marked by punctuation of some sort, or may simply be a natural pause occasioned by the rhythm of the language used. It may come anywhere in the line but is most often in the middle. Ten syllable lines often have a cæsura and such pauses are very useful for poets wishing to vary the otherwise monotonous effect of strict **iamb**ic **pentameter.** Shakespeare was a master of the use of cæsuras in his blank verse plays, thus reproducing natural speech rhythms within the iambic lines. However, cæsuras can be found in all metres, but less so in the very shortest, such as **dimeter.**

Examples:

1. From *Adlestrop* by Edward Thomas

Yes. I remember Adlestrop –
The name, because one afternoon
Of heat the express-train drew up there
Unwontedly. It was late June.

Although the underlying rhythm is iambic **tetrameter,** the cæsuras in each line (after *Yes, name, heat* and *Unwontedly*) mean that the poem reads more conversationally.

In the example that follows there are cæsuras in lines 3 and 5 by punctuation, and also in line 4 after *gives.*

2. *The Merchant of Venice*, Act 4, Scene 1 by William Shakespeare

The quality of mercy is not strain'd;
It droppeth as the gentle rain from heaven
Upon the place beneath. It is twice blest:
It blesseth him that gives and him that takes.
'Tis mightiest in the mightiest; it becomes
The throned monarch better than his crown;

DACTYL

DACTYL (pronounced DAC-til) A dactyl is a metrical **foot** of three syllables – long, short, short (dum-di-di, usually shown as ⁄ ⌣ ⌣). The stress comes on the first syllable, as in the words *lucki*ly, *fore*ster, *capi*tal, *inter*view and *senti*ment. It takes its name from the Greek word meaning 'finger', from the strong joint (at the knuckle) followed by two weaker ones. Verse written predominantly in this metre would be called dactylic (pronounced dac-TIL-ic). It produces a 'falling rhythm' which is not a natural rhythm of spoken English. However, as with many classical techniques, it was revived and used by a number of nineteenth century poets.

Examples:

1. From *The Bridge of Sighs* by Thomas Hood

```
  ⁄     ᴗ   ᴗ | ⁄   ᴗ  ᴗ
```

One more Unfortunate,
Weary of breath,
Rashly importunate,
Gone to her death!
Take her up tenderly,
Lift her with care;
Fashion'd so slenderly
Young, and so fair!

Look at her garments
Clinging like cerements;
Whilst the wave constantly
Drips from her clothing;
Take her up instantly,
Loving, not loathing

2. From *The Voice* by Thomas Hardy

```
  ⁄   ᴗ   ᴗ  | ⁄     ᴗ    ᴗ | ⁄  ᴗ  ᴗ  | ⁄  ᴗ  ᴗ
```

Woman much missed, how you call to me, call to me,
Saying that now you are not what you were
When you had changed from the one who was all to me,
But as at first when our day was fair.

DIMETER
Dimeter is the name given to a line of just two feet – two strong stresses. The feet may be of any kind – **iamb**ic, **trocha**ic, **dactyl**ic, **anapæst**ic etc. (see **foot**). This well-known nursery rhyme is an example of trochaic dimeter (dum-di / dum-di).

Example:

Tinker, tailor,
Soldier, sailor,

Rich man, poor man,
Beggar-man, thief.

Not many poems are written entirely in such short lines, but may contain dimeter as part of the structure of stanzas. The following is an example of iambic dimeter (di-dum / di-dum) in the second and fourth lines of each stanza, highlighted here in italics.

From *Who's in the Next Room?* by Thomas Hardy

'Who's in the next room? – who?
   I seemed to see
Somebody in the dawning passing through,
   Unknown to me.'
'Nay: you saw nought. He passed invisibly.'

'Who's in the next room? – who?
   I seem to hear
Somebody muttering firm in a language new
   That chills the ear.'
'No: you catch not his tongue who has entered there.'

In the following poem each line contains a **dactyl** (dum-di-di) and either a **trochee** (dum-di) or a one syllable foot (dum), in this case, a truncated trochee.

Example:

From *The Water-Nymph and the Boy* by the Hon. Roden Noel (1834–94)

Father and mother,
Weeping and wild,
Came to the forest,
Calling the child,
Came from the palace,
Down to the pool,
Calling my darling,
My beautiful!
Under the water,
Cold and so pale!
Could it be love made
Beauty to fail?

FEMININE ENDING
A line of verse is said to have a feminine ending if the last word ends on an unstressed syllable. This may also be known as a weak ending. (History has equated feminine with weak! No single syllable words are ever feminine, instead they are known as strong or **masculine ending**s.) However, two, three, or more syllable words where the stress is not on the last syllable are always feminine. Examples of such words are: *under, over, after, Sunday* (two syllables); *discover, submissive, exhausted, carrying* (three syllables); *subordinate, disconcerting, activity, convenient* (four syllables); *cafeteria, supernatural, insignificant, impersonating* (five syllables); *alphabetically, unimaginative* (six syllables) etc.

You frequently find such endings in **blank verse** which may have a weak or feminine ending giving an eleventh syllable to an otherwise strictly ten syllable line.

Examples:

1. *Hamlet*, Act 3, Scene 1 by William Shakespeare
To be, or not to be – that is the question;
Whether 'tis nobler in the mind to suffer
The slings and arrows of outrageous fortune . . .

In the following poem lines 1, 3, 5 and 7 have feminine rhyme endings (*highland* and *island*, *encloses* and *roses*) whilst the alternate lines 2, 4, 6 and 8 have **masculine ending**s (*lee* and *sea*, *bed* and *dead*).

2. From *A Forsaken Garden* by Algernon Charles Swinburne
In a coign of the cliff between lowland and highland,
At the sea-down's edge between windward and lee,
Walled round with rocks is an inland island,
The ghost of a garden fronts the sea.
A girdle of brushwood and thorn encloses
The steep square slope of the blossomless bed
Where the leaves that grew green from the graves of its roses
Now lie dead.

FOOT
A foot is a unit of rhythm made up of a number of stressed and unstressed syllables. It is rather like a bar in music in that a set number of feet will make a line of poetry just as a set number of bars will make a line of a song. There are well over 20 different

kinds of feet but only five are really common in English verse. Here they are in order of popular use: **iamb, trochee, dactyl, anapæst** and **spondee**.

A foot is measured by the pattern and number of syllables – long or stressed syllables are shown by the symbol ´; short or unstressed syllables are shown by the symbol ˘.

The Feet

1. Iamb (di-dum or ˘ ´) as in the words be*hind*, de*cide* and re*lax*.

2. Trochee (dum-di or ´ ˘) as in the words *und*er, *sof*a and *saun*ter.

3. Dactyl (dum-di-di or ´ ˘ ˘) as in the words *for*ester, *syll*able and *cap*ital.

4. Anapæst (di-di-dum or ˘ ˘ ´) as in the phrases in a *wood*, up a*bove* and have a *go*.

5. Spondee (dum-dum or ´ ´) as in the phrases *stand still*, *sea breeze* and *you too*.

Occasionally other feet will also occur in English verse:

6. Amphibrach (di-dum-di or ˘ ´ ˘) as in the words in*sid*er, re*volt*ing and de*light*ful.

7. Pæon (dum-di-di-di or di-dum-di-di or di-di-dum-di or di-di-di-dum) a foot with one stressed and three unstressed syllables which can be in any order.

(see individual entries for examples)

HEPTAMETER (pronounced hept-AM-eter) A heptameter is a line of verse containing seven feet – seven strong stresses (see **foot** and **metre**). It might be compared to a line of a song containing seven bars, each with one strong beat. It was used by Latin and Greek poets but has not been a popular line-length for English writers. Because it has seven feet, it is the same metre as folk ballads tend to be where the seven beats spread over two lines – four beats and then three.

In the following example, the seven feet of each heptameter line are a mixture of **iambic** (di-dum), **anapæstic** (di-di-dum) and **dactylic** rhythm (dum-di-di).

Example:

The Market-Girl by Thomas Hardy

Nobody took any notice of her as she stood on the causey kerb,
All eager to sell her honey and apples and bunches of garden
herb;
And if she had offered to give her wares and herself with them
too that day,
I doubt if a soul would have cared to take a bargain so choice
away.

But chancing to trace her sunburnt grace that morning as I
passed nigh,
I went and I said 'Poor maidy dear! – and will none of the people
buy?'
And so it began; and soon we knew what the end of it all must
be,
And I found that though no others had bid, a prize had been
won by me.

- -

HEXAMETER (pronounced hex-AM-eter) A hexameter is a line

of verse containing six feet – six strong stresses (see **foot** and **metre**).
It might be compared to a line of a song containing six bars, each
with one strong beat. It is the line-length of an **alexandrine** which
is written in **iamb**ic hexameter. The English language is more suited
to the iambic **pentameter**, and few poets have chosen to write using
the hexameter line. **Dactyl**ic hexameter was, however, the metre of
Latin and Greek epic verse, whilst other languages, notably French,
have employed the alexandrine. These are principally languages
whose structure and grammar usually require more syllables to say
what English can accomplish in fewer.

The following poems are examples of the use of hexameters. The
first example is in iambic hexameter, while in the second only the
last lines of each stanza are hexameters.

Examples:

1. *Trust thou thy Love* by John Ruskin

∪ ／ | ∪ ／ |∪ ／ |∪ ／ |∪ ／ | ∪ ／
Trust thou thy Love: if she be proud, is she not sweet?

Trust thou thy Love: if she be mute, is she not pure?
Lay thou thy soul full in her hands, low at her feet;
Fail, Sun and Breath! – yet, for thy peace, She shall endure.

2. From *To a Skylark* by Percy Bysshe Shelley

Hail to thee, blithe spirit!
Bird thou never wert –
That from heaven or near it
Pourest thy full heart
In profuse strains of unpremeditated art.

. . .

Teach me half the gladness
That thy brain must know;
Such harmonious madness
From my lips would flow,
The world should listen then, as I am listening now.

IAMB
(pronounced EYE-am) **iambic** (adjective, pronounced eye-AM-bic). An iamb is a metrical **foot** of two syllables with the first weak or unstressed, and the second strong or stressed (di-dum or ᴗ ╱). It takes its name from a Greek word and means 'the limping rhythm' (try limping round the room to feel the rhythm). It is the most common rhythm in English poetry as it is very close to normal speech patterns.

In the following example lines alternate between iambic **tetrameter** or four iambic feet and iambic **trimeter** or three iambic feet.

Examples:

1. *How Doth the Little Crocodile* by Lewis Carroll

   ᴗ   ╱ | ᴗ ╱|ᴗ ╱|ᴗ╱
How doth the little crocodile
   ᴗ ╱ | ᴗ ╱ | ᴗ ╱
Improve his shining tail,
And pour the waters of the Nile
On every golden scale!

How cheerfully he seems to grin,
How neatly spreads his claws,

And welcomes little fishes in,
With gently smiling jaws.

The next extract is an example of iambic **pentameter** or five iambic feet (see also **blank verse**).

2. From *Julius Caesar*, Act 1, Scene 2 by William Shakespeare

˘ ′ | ˘ ′ | ˘ ′ | ˘ ′ | ˘ ′

Cassius: Why, man, he doth bestride the narrow world
Like a Colossus, and we petty men
Walk under his huge legs, and peep about
To find ourselves dishonourable graves.
Men at some time are masters of their fates:
The fault, dear Brutus, is not in our stars,
But in ourselves, that we are underlings.

MASCULINE ENDING

A line of verse is said to have a masculine ending if the last word ends on a stressed syllable. This is also known as a strong ending. All single syllable words are, therefore, masculine or strong (see also **feminine ending**). Words such as *hope, trust, before, decide, understand, episode, identified* and *mythology* are masculine as the final syllable is stressed.
The following poem uses masculine rhymes to end each line.

Example:

Cock-Crow by Edward Thomas
Out of the wood of thoughts that grows by night
To be cut down by the sharp axe of light, –
Out of the night, two cocks together crow,
Cleaving the darkness with a silver blow:
And bright before my eyes twin trumpeters stand,
Heralds of splendour, one at either hand,
Each facing each, as in a coat of arms:
The milkers lace their boots up at the farms.

METRE

Metre is the **rhythm**, or pattern of stressed and unstressed syllables, of a line of verse. Metrical verse is written in feet, or units of rhythm, arranged in patterns (see **foot**). The feet most used in English verse are the **iamb, trochee, anapæst, dactyl, spondee, amphibrach** and **pæon.**

Metre also refers to the length of a line, which will vary according to the number of feet used. The following are the terms for the different line-lengths: one foot = **monometer,** two feet = **dimeter,** three feet = **trimeter,** four feet = **tetrameter,** five feet = **pentameter,** six feet = **hexameter,** seven feet = **heptameter** and eight feet = **octameter.**

(see also **sprung rhythm, scansion** and **free verse**)

MONOMETER Monometer is the term for a line of verse containing only one **foot.** In English verse monometer is not common for a whole poem but may occur at intervals within a poem predominantly written in another **metre.**

The monometer lines, highlighted in the following poem in italics, are mostly, though not exclusively, **anapæstic.**

Example:

> **From *A Song About Myself* by John Keats**
> There was a naughty Boy,
> And a naughty Boy was he,
> He ran away to Scotland
> The people for to see
> *Then he found*
> *That the ground*
> *Was as hard,*
> *That a yard*
> *Was as long,*
> *That a song*
> *Was as merry,*
> *That a cherry*
> *Was as red –*
> *That lead*
> *Was as weighty,*
> *That fourscore*
> *Was as eighty,*
> *That a door*

Was as wooden
As in England –
And he wonder'd
He wonder'd
He stood in his shoes
And he wonder'd.

OCTAMETER
Octameter is the term for a line of verse containing eight feet in any combination – eight strong stresses (see **foot** and **metre**). This length of line is rare in English verse; such a line would be more likely to be split into two lines of **tetrameter** as this metre is more suited to English language rhythms.

The third line of the stanza in the following poem is in octameter.

Example:

From *O Come Quickly!* by Thomas Campion
Never weather-beaten sail more willing bent to shore,
Never tired pilgrim's limbs affected slumber more,
Then my weary spright now longs to fly out of my troubled
  breast.
O! come quickly, sweetest Lord, and take my soul to rest.

PÆON
A pæon is a **foot** of one stressed syllable and three unstressed syllables.

These may come in any order, either dum-di-di-di (known as the first pæon because the stress is on the first syllable) or di-dum-di-di (the second pæon) or di-di-dum-di (the third pæon) or di-di-di-dum (the fourth pæon). It is rarely used in English verse except for **sprung rhythm**.

PENTAMETER
Pentameter is the term for a line of verse containing five feet in any combination – five strong stresses (see **foot** and **metre**). The pentameter is a very common and popular line-length in English verse – see particularly **blank verse**, **iamb** and **heroic couplet**. The following extract is an example of iambic pentameter, with a minor variation of rhythm in the last line.

Example:

***In Memoriam* (*Easter, 1915*) by Edward Thomas**

The flowers left thick at nightfall in the wood
This Eastertide call into mind the men,
Now far from home, who, with their sweethearts, should
Have gathered them and will do never again.

RHYTHM

Rhythm is the pattern of stressed and unstressed syllables which make up a line of verse or a whole poem (see **metre**).

SCANSION

Scansion is the method of analysing the **rhythm** or **metre** of a line of metrical verse. Metrical verse is written in patterns of feet (see **foot**), and for each foot the stressed syllables are usually marked above with the symbol /, while the unstressed syllables are marked with the symbol ⌣. We talk about 'scanning' a line, from the verb 'to scan'. Each foot is separated on the scansion line with the symbol | .

The following is an example of **iamb**ic **pentameter** (five feet) – here it is a closed **heroic couplet**.

Examples:

1. Attributed to Orlando Gibbons

⌣ /| ⌣ / | ⌣ /| ⌣ / |⌣ /
The silver swan, who living had no note,
⌣ / | ⌣ / | ⌣ / | ⌣ /| ⌣ /
When death approached unlocked her silent throat;

The next extract is an example of **tetrameter** (four feet), alternating two **trochee** with two monosyllabic feet.

2. *A Midsummer Night's Dream*, Act 2, Scene 1 by William Shakespeare

/ ⌣| /||/ ⌣| /
Over hill, over dale,
/ ⌣ | / || / ⌣ | /
Thorough bush, thorough brier,
/ ⌣| / ||/ ⌣/ /
Over park, over pale,
/ ⌣ | / || / ⌣ |/
Thorough flood, thorough fire

SPONDEE
A spondee is a metrical **foot** containing two stressed syllables. English verse would not generally be written entirely in spondees (as it often <u>is</u> entirely in **iamb**s) but the occasional spondee will occur in lines predominantly in other **metre**s. The spondee slows the rhythm of a line down, making it heavier or more jagged, and poets will use it to create a particular effect.

In the following extract, the spondees are highlighted in italics.

Example:

From *Dulce et Decorum Est* by Wilfred Owen
Bent double, like old beggars under sacks,
Knock-kneed, coughing like hags, we cursed through sludge,
Till on the haunting flares we turned our backs
And towards our distant rest began to trudge.
Men marched asleep. Many had lost their boots
But *limped on*, *blood-shod*. All went lame; all blind;
Drunk with fatigue; deaf even to the hoots
Of gas shells dropping softly behind.

Gas! Gas! Quick, boys! – An ecstasy of fumbling,
Fitting the clumsy helmets just in time;

SPRUNG RHYTHM
Sprung rhythm is the term invented by Gerard Manley Hopkins to describe the metrical movement of his verse. Sprung rhythm as such was not invented by him but had existed in English poetry since the time of the Anglo-Saxons who frequently used such rhythms. Indeed, Hopkins acknowledged his debt to Anglo-Saxon alliterative poetry, but his coining of the term has become the accepted name for what he described as an 'abrupt' rhythm. It has been influential among many twentieth century poets, such as T. S. Eliot, Ted Hughes and Dylan Thomas.

The Form
● Each foot contains from one to four syllables, often with other added unstressed syllables.

● Each foot has one strong stress on the first syllable.

- The feet that can be used are: a monosyllable, a **trochee**, a **dactyl** and a **pæon** (with strong stress on the first syllable).

- These feet can be used in any order or combination in a line. There may often be a succession of monosyllables – one strong stress after another.

- The **scansion** of a line may 'rove over' (in Gerard Manley Hopkins' own words). This means that if one line ends with one or more unstressed syllables, the following line will begin with that many fewer. Also, if one line ends on a strong stress, the next may begin with one or more weak syllables. The scansion of sprung rhythm should be taken as a whole over the poem, rather than line by line as in other English verse.

Example:

Pied Beauty by Gerard Manley Hopkins

Glory be to God for dappled things –
For skies of couple-colour as a brinded cow;
For rose-moles all in stipple upon trout that swim;
Fresh-firecoal chestnut-falls; finches' wings;
Landscape plotted and pieced – fold, fallow, and plough;
And áll trádes, their gear and tackle and trim.

All things counter, original, spare, strange;
Whatever is fickle, freckled (who knows how?)
With swift, slow; sweet, sour; adazzle, dim;
He fathers-forth whose beauty is past change:
Praise him.

SYLLABIC VERSE
Syllabic verse is poetry measured by the number of syllables in each line rather than by any metre or rhyme. Many poets in the 1950s and 1960s experimented with syllabic verse, choosing their own number of syllables per line, and this may read like **free verse** but it is not the same. There are specific syllabic forms, many of which have been introduced into English verse from Japanese poetry, whose forms are determined entirely by a set number of syllables per line (see **cinquain, haiku, naga-uta, renga** and **tanka**).

TETRAMETER
Tetrameter is the term given to a line of verse containing four feet of any kind – four strong stresses (see **foot** and **metre**).

Example:

From *To His Coy Mistress* by Andrew Marvell

˘ ´ | ˘ ´ | ˘ ´ | ˘ ´

Had we but world enough, and time,
This coyness, Lady, were no crime.
We would sit down and think which way
To walk and pass our long love's day.

TRIMETER
Trimeter is the term for a line of verse containing three feet of any kind – three strong stresses (see **foot** and **metre**).

Example:

Heredity by Thomas Hardy

´ ˘ ˘ | ´ ˘ ˘ | ´

I am the family face;
Flesh perishes, I live on,
Projecting trait and trace
Through time to times anon,
And leaping from place to place
Over oblivion.

The years-heired feature that can
In curve and voice and eye
Despise the human span
Of durance – that is I;
The eternal thing in man,
That heeds no call to die.

TROCHEE
(pronouced TRO-key) Trochee is a metrical **foot** of one stressed syllable followed by an unstressed syllable – dum-di. It is also sometimes called the falling rhythm and is the opposite of an **iamb**. Although not much English verse is written completely in trochaic metre, the trochee is often used in **blank verse** to relieve what can otherwise become the monotonous effect of a strictly iambic line. The following extract is entirely in trochaic metre.

Examples:

1. From *Hiawatha* by Henry Wadsworth Longfellow

Swift of foot was Hiawatha;
He could shoot an arrow from him,
And run forward with such fleetness,
That the arrow fell behind him!

Strong of arm was Hiawatha;
He could shoot ten arrows upward,
Shoot them with such strength and swiftness,
That the tenth had left the bowstring
Ere the first to earth had fallen!

The first three lines in the next example are basically trochaic, but the fourth line changes to the iambic – an iamb being the mirror image of a trochee.

2. From *The Tiger* by William Blake

/ ⏑ | / ⏑ | / ⏑ | /
Tiger! Tiger! burning bright
/ ⏑ | / ⏑ | / ⏑ | /
In the forests of the night
/ ⏑ | / ⏑ | / ⏑ | /
What immortal hand or eye
⏑ / | ⏑ / | ⏑ / | ⏑ /
Could frame thy fearful symmetry?

VERSE

A Midsummer Night's Dream, Act 5, Scene 1

The poet's eye, in a fine frenzy rolling,
Doth glance from heaven to earth, from earth to heaven;
And as imagination bodies forth
The forms of things unknown, the poet's pen
Turns them to shapes, and gives to airy nothing
A local habitation and a name.

William Shakespeare

*ACROSTIC

*ACROSTIC An acrostic is a poem in which letters on successive lines spell a word when read downwards. The most common form is where the first letters of each line make the word, which is often also the subject of the poem.

Example:

> **A**crostics are popular poems to write,
> **C**hildren, especially, experience delight.
> **R**hyming, of course, they usually forgo,
> **O**pting for easy ways out; although
> **S**ome don't remember when they commence
> **T**hat acrostic poems have to make sense.
> **I**nitial letters should make you think hard,
> **C**arefully choose what to keep or discard –
> **S**o your final poem is viewed with regard.
>
> **SB**

If the middle letters of each line form the word this is called a *mesostich*; if it is the end letters of each line the poem is called a *telestich*.

*ALCAIC VERSE Alcaic verse is called after the Greek poet, Alkaios, and is a **stanza** form of a **quatrain** (four lines) written predominantly in **dactyl**ic metre. It is not much used in English verse but several of the Victorian poets, such as Algernon Charles Swinburne, Alfred, Lord Tennyson and Robert Louis Stevenson, enjoyed experimenting with the form.

The Form

- The stanza form is of four lines – a quatrain, and any number of stanzas may be used for the poem.

- It is predominantly written in dactylic metre (dum-di-di), although there will be variations at times, usually using **trochee** (dum-di) or a monosyllable **foot** (dum).

- It is not rhymed.

The following extract is both dactylic and trochaic.

Example:

From *Milton* by Alfred, Lord Tennyson

╱ ◡ ◡| ╱   ◡| ╱ ◡ ◡| ╱   ◡ ◡
O mighty-mouth'd inventor of harmonies,
O skill'd to I sing of I Time or E I ternity,
God-gifted I organ-I voice of I England,
Milton, a I name to re I sound for I ages;

*BALLAD A ballad is a poem that tells a story which was originally composed in the form of a song. Folk ballads were handed down orally and so versions often varied in different parts of the country. Many of these were first written down by Cecil Sharp (1859–1924), the English collector of folk songs and dances, in the latter half of the nineteenth century and the early part of the twentieth century. Most ballads are anonymous.

The Form

● Four lines (a **quatrain**), usually rhyming a,b,c,b but sometimes a,b,a,b.

● The first and third lines have four beats or stresses (four feet = **tetrameter**).

● The second and fourth lines have three beats or stresses (three feet = **trimeter**).

● Occasionally there is a **refrain** – one or more repeated lines.

Examples:

1. From *The Unquiet Grave*

Cold blows the wind tonight, sweetheart,
Cold are the drops of *rain*;
I never had but one true love
And in greenwood he lies *slain*.

2. From *Barbara Allen's Cruelty*

All in the merry month of *May*,
When green buds they were *swellin'*,
Young Jemmy Grove on his death-bed *lay*,
For love of Barbara *Allen*.

3. From *A Lyke-Wake Dirge*

This ae nighte, this ae nighte,
– *Every nighte and alle,*　　　　　(refrain each stanza)
Fire and fleet and candle-lighte,
And Christe receive thy saule.　　(refrain each stanza)
(fleet = house-room)

The Literary Ballad

The literary ballad is a poem created in the style of the folk ballads. Several writers imitated such story poems and they used many of the same devices, though not always as strictly as the originals. Probably the most famous of these are: Samuel Taylor Coleridge's *Rime of the Ancient Mariner*; John Keats' *La Belle Dame sans Merci*; Oscar Wilde's *The Ballad of Reading Gaol*, and Rudyard Kipling's *Barrack Room Ballads*.

Examples:

1. From *La Belle Dame sans Merci* by John Keats

'O what can ail thee, knight-at-arms,
　　Alone and palely loitering?
The sedge is withered from the lake,
　　And no birds sing.'

2. From *Rime of the Ancient Mariner* by Samuel Taylor Coleridge

The thick black cloud was cleft, and still
The Moon was at its side;
Like waters shot from some high crag,
The lightning fell with never a jag,
A river steep and wide.

The loud wind never reach'd the ship,
Yet now the ship moved on!
Beneath the lightning and the Moon
The dead men gave a groan.

*BALLADE (pronounced ba-LARD) A ballade is an Old French form which was popular in the fourteenth and fifteenth centuries. The strictness of the form, with its few rhymes, has meant that it has enjoyed only limited success with poets writing in the English

language. Chaucer used the form occasionally, and it was revived by some Victorian poets, such as Algernon Charles Swinburne and W.E. Henley. In more recent times, in the earlier part of the twentieth century, it has been used for lighter verse by G.K. Chesterton and Hilaire Belloc, among others.

When attempting to write a ballade it is essential to choose rhymes from words which offer many other possible rhymes. This is not so easy in English. Depending on the type of ballade tried, up to 14 rhymes on the same sound will be needed!

The Most Common Form of Ballade:

- Three eight-line **stanza**s followed by an **envoi** of four lines. The envoi was generally addressed to someone, such as a patron.

- Each line was supposed to have eight syllables, but English poets usually deviate from this.

- The last line of the first stanza becomes the **refrain** (C – see below under rhyme scheme) and is repeated at the end of each successive stanza and the envoi.

- The rhyme scheme is a,b,a,b,b,c,b,C (for each stanza) and b,c,b,C (for the envoi).

Example:

Ballade of Dead Actors **by W.E. Henley**

Where are the passions they essayed,	a
And where the tears they made to flow?	b
Where the wild humours they portrayed	a
For laughing worlds to see and know?	b
Othello's wrath and Juliet's woe?	b
Sir Peter's whims and Timon's gall?	c
And Millamant and Romeo?	b
Into the night go one and all.	**C**
Where are the braveries, fresh and frayed?	a
The plumes, the armours – friend and foe?	b
The cloth of gold, the rare brocade,	a
The mantles glittering to and fro?	b
The pomp, the pride, the royal show?	b
The cries of war and festival?	c

| The youth, the grace, the charm, the glow? | b |
| Into the night go one and all. | **C** |

The curtain falls, the play is played:	a
The Beggar packs beside the Beau;	b
The Monarch troops, and troops the Maid;	a
The Thunder huddles with the Snow.	b
Where are the revellers high and low?	b
The clashing swords? The lover's call?	c
The dancers gleaming row on row?	b
Into the night go one and all.	**C**

Envoy

Prince, in one common overthrow	b
The Hero tumbles with the Thrall:	c
As dust that drives, as straws that blow,	b
Into the night go one and all.	**C**

This second example is more typical of the light verse tradition in English ballades and shows the poet allowing himself some leeway and adjusting the form to suit his needs. With its reference to Darwin's theories published in his work, *Origin of Species*, it serves as a comment on nineteenth century society and, indeed, on any age.

Example:

A Ballade of Evolution by Grant Allen (1848–1899)

In the mud of the Cambrian main
Did our earliest ancestor dive:
From a shapeless albuminous grain
We mortals our being derive.
He could split himself up into five,
Or roll himself round like a ball;
For the fittest will always survive,
While the weakliest go to the wall.

As an active ascidian again
Fresh forms he began to contrive,
Till he grew to a fish with a brain,
And brought forth a mammal alive.
With his rivals he next had to strive
To woo him a mate and a thrall;

So the handsomest managed to wive,
While the ugliest went to the wall.

At length as an ape he was fain
The nuts of the forest to rive,
Till he took to the low-lying plain,
And proceeded his fellows to knive.
Thus did cannibal men first arrive
One another to swallow and maul:
And the strongest continued to thrive,
While the weakliest went to the wall.

> Envoy

Prince, in our civilised hive,
Now money's the measure of all;
And the wealthy in coaches can drive,
While the needier go to the wall.

A Second Type of Ballade:

- Three ten-line stanzas followed by a five-line or six-line envoi.

- Each line has ten syllables, usually written in **iamb**ic **pentameter**.

- The last line of the first stanza becomes the refrain (**D** – see rhyme scheme below) and is repeated at the end of each successive stanza and the envoi.

- The rhyme scheme is a,b,a,b,b,c,c,d,c,**D** for each stanza and c,c,d,c,**D** (for the five-line envoi) or c,c,d,c,c,**D** (for the six-line envoi).

The Double Ballade

- Six eight-line or ten-line stanzas; there may be an envoi, but this is often left out.

- It has the same rhyme scheme as the common ballade.

The Double-Refrain Ballade

- This has the same form as the common ballade but has two refrains – at line 4 (**B**) and line 8 (**C**).

- Thus the rhyme scheme is as follows: a,b,a,**B**,b,c,b,**C** (for each stanza) and b,**B**,c,**C** (for the envoi).

The Ballade Royal

- Geoffrey Chaucer wrote some poems in this form, using three or four seven-line stanzas with no envoi (see **rhyme royal**).

- Each line may have either eight syllables (written in iambic **tetrameter**) or ten syllables (written in iambic pentameter).

- The last line of each stanza is the repeated refrain (**C** – see rhyme scheme below).

- The rhyme scheme is a,b,a,b,b,c,**C**.

Example:

Balade by Geoffrey Chaucer

Hide, Absalom, thy gilte tresses clear;	a
Esther, lay thou thy meekness all a-down;	b
Hide, Jonathan, all thy friendly mannér;	a
Penelope and Marcia Catóun	b
Make of your wifehood no comparisón;	b
Hide ye your beauties, Isolde and Elaine:	c
My lady com'th, that all this may distain.	**C**
Thy faire body let it not appear,	a
Lavine; and thou, Lucrece of Rome town,	b
And Polixene, that boughten love so dear,	a
And Cleopatre, with all thy passión,	b
Hide ye your truth of love and your renown;	b
And thou, Thisbe, that hast for love such pain:	c
My lady com'th, that all this may distain.	**C**
Hero, Dido, Leodámia, all y-ferer,	a
And Phyllis, hanging for thy Demophon,	b
And Cánacé, espièd by thy chere,	a
Hypsípylé, betraysèd with Jasón,	b
Make of your truthe neither boast nor soun;	b
Nor Hypermestre or Ariadne, ye twain:	c
My lady com'th, that all this may distain.	**C**

*CALLIGRAM

A calligram (or calligramme) is a form of **concrete poetry**. The poem is set out in a shape on the page and its success depends largely upon its visual effect. Thus, it is often more a question of design and typography than of poetry. Calligrams are difficult to do well as the words and layout need to interact with each other. Too often, it seems, poems are written in shapes just for the sake of a different kind of presentation.

One of the best-known and successful writers of calligrams in the twentieth century was the French poet, Apollinaire. However, poets have experimented with shape poems for hundreds of years. The Greek poet, Simmias of Rhodes, (circa 324 BC) wrote poems in the shape of wings, an egg and a hatchet. Among English poets, George Herbert, writing in the seventeenth century, is famous for two poems, *Easter Wings* and *The Altar*. Perhaps even better known is *The Mouse's Tale* by Lewis Carroll in *Alice's Adventures in Wonderland*, written in the form of a mouse's tail. The following example is by a Hindu poet. It consists of three lines (a rhyming **triplet**) which together form a bow and arrow. The arrow is the final line which is aimed at the poet's desired lady.

One kiss I send, to pierce like fire thy too reluctant heart.

O lovely maid, thou art the fairest slave in all God's mart!

Those charms to win, with all my empire I would gladly part

CHAIN VERSE

Chain verse is a term given to verse which is linked from **stanza** to stanza in some way, either by rhyme or by repetition of syllables, words or phrases. Examples of verse using linked rhyming which carries over from one stanza to the next, would be **Spenserian sonnet**s, the **Spenserian stanza** and **terza rima**. Other forms, such as the **villanelle, rondeau** and **pantoum**, repeat whole lines on a set pattern across the stanzas. Chain verse is also evident in poems where the last syllable of a line is repeated in the first syllable of the next. The sound of each syllable should be the same but the meaning should be different. This is rare in English verse, although there are examples of poems where the last word or phrase of a line is repeated as the first word or phrase of the following line (see also **echo verse**).

*CHANT ROYAL

The chant royal is a French poetic form from the Middle Ages. It is related to the ballade but is principally used to deal with serious subjects. It has a strict rhyme scheme, a **refrain** and an **envoi**.

The Form

● Five eleven-line **stanza**s followed by an envoi of five lines, a total of 60 lines in all.

● Each stanza has the following rhyme scheme: a,b,a,b,c,c,d,d,e,d,E (**E** = the refrain).

● The envoi rhymes d,d,e,d,**E**.

● No rhyme word may be used more than once, except in the envoi.

Clearly, with so many rhymes on one sound required, this form is not ideally suited to the English language and few English poets have experimented with chant royal. There was a revival of interest in such older forms during the Victorian era but chant royal never really became popular.

*CINQUAIN

(pronounced SIN-kwain or SAN-kan) A cinquain is the general term for any five-line **stanza**, irrespective of its rhythm or rhyme scheme. In the Middle Ages, it was also known as a quintain. However, nowadays, a cinquain almost always refers to the specific syllabic form invented by an American poet, Adelaide Crapsey (1878–1914).

The Form

● Five lines written predominantly in **iamb**ic **rhythm.**

● It does not rhyme but is based on a set number of syllables per line, as follows: two in the first line; four in the second; six in the third; eight in the fourth, and two in the fifth (2, 4, 6, 8, 2).

● The poem builds as each line becomes longer until the last line which, being suddenly short, allows particular emphasis to fall on the words and meaning of the ending.

Examples:

1. *November Night* by Adelaide Crapsey

Listen ...	2
With faint dry sound,	4
Like steps of passing ghosts,	6
The leaves, frost-crisp'd, break from the trees	8
And fall.	2

2. *The Warning* by Adelaide Crapsey

Just now,
Out of the strange
Still dusk – as strange, as still –
A white moth flew. Why am I grown
So cold?

*CLERIHEW

Clerihews are named after the inventor of the form, Edmund Clerihew Bentley (1875–1956). He is said to have written his first clerihew about Sir Humphrey Davy, while still at school during a boring chemistry lesson. A clerihew is intended to be a short witty comment on a biographical aspect of a famous person's character or life.

The Form

● Four lines (a **quatrain**) rhyming a,a,b,b.

● The first line usually consists only of the name of the person who is the subject of the clerihew.

● Lines can be of varying length and rhythm (this can enhance the humour).

Examples:

1. Hitler
Was considerably littler
And less endowed than other males,
According to the popular tales.

SB

2. Elizabeth the First
Was said to thirst
For Essex in bed,
But remained unwed.

SB

CONCRETE POETRY

Concrete poetry is principally a visual poetry which relies on typography and layout, as well as words, to make its effect (see **calligram**). In more recent times other kinds of experimental verse have been included under the general heading of concrete poetry. Among these would be sound poetry which uses letters and combinations of letters, more often than words, and is chanted or intoned as a kind of mouth and mood music. This is not a very popular or prevalent kind of poetry.

COUPLET

COUPLET A couplet is two successive lines of verse which are usually of the same **rhythm** or **metre**. Couplets most often rhyme, but not always. A poem may be written in a series of couplets, either free-standing or in sequences making up longer **stanza**s (see also **heroic couplet**).

Examples:

1. From *Alice Through the Looking-Glass* by Lewis Carroll

I sent a message to the fish:
I told them, 'This is what I wish.'

The little fishes of the sea,
They sent an answer back to me.

The little fishes' answer was
'We cannot do it, Sir, because –'

2. From *The Clock-Winder* by Thomas Hardy

It is dark as a cave,
Or a vault in the nave
When the iron door
Is closed, and the floor
Of the church relaid
With trowel and spade.
But the parish-clerk
Cares not for the dark
As he winds in the tower
At a regular hour
The rheumatic clock
Whose dilatory knock
You can hear when praying
At the day's decaying,
Or at any lone while
From a pew in the aisle.

3. The train that has arrived at platform one
Will leave when it is ready, not before.

All passengers who wish to take this train
Must claim their one-way ticket from the guard.

Its destination will remain unknown,
And every empty seat has been reserved.

Provision has been made for sleeping cars
We guarantee you'll sleep dead to the world.

SB

DOGGEREL Doggerel originally described verse written in an irregular metre. Nowadays it generally refers to badly written verse, often in **couplet**s or **quatrain**s, which is not well-crafted, does not scan, and whose rhymes can be very banal. It is often unintentionally humorous as in the work of the best-known example of such versifiers, the Scottish writer, William McGonagall.

Examples:

1. From *A Summary History of Lord Clive* by William McGonagall

And all the greatest people in the land
Were proud to shake him by the hand;
And they gave him a beautiful sword because he had fought so
    well
And of his bravery the people to each other did tell.

And when his own friends saw him they to him ran,
And they hardly knew him, he looked so noble a man;
And his parents felt o'erjoyed when they saw him home again,
And when he left his parents again for India it caused them great
    pain.

But it was a good thing Clive returned to India again,
Because a wicked prince in his territory wouldn't allow the British
    to remain,
And he resolved to drive them off his land,
And marched upon them boldly with thousands of his band.

Doggerel can work better, however, when it is used intentionally for comic or satirical comment.

2. *Higher Education* Anon

As I was laying on the green
A little book it chanced I seen.
Carlyle's *Essay on Burns* was the edition –
I left it laying in the same position.

3. *Napoleon* Anon

Napoleon hoped that all the world would fall beneath his sway;
He failed in his ambition; and where is he today?
Neither the nations of the East nor the nations of the West
Have thought the thing Napoleon thought was to their interest.

*ECHO VERSE

Echo verse is poetry in which the last syllables of a line are repeated (like an echo) but with a change of meaning. The poem is rather like a dialogue with the echo commenting on what has gone before. It was a popular device in poetry of the sixteenth, seventeenth and eighteenth centuries, both for religious verse (notably George Herbert) and often for satirical verse.

Examples:

1. From *Heaven* by George Herbert

What leaves are they? impart the matter wholly.
       Echo.   *Holy*
Are holy leaves the Echo then of bliss?
       Echo. *Yes.*
Then tell me, what is that supreme delight?
       Echo. *Light.*
Light to the mind: what shall the will enjoy?
       Echo. *Joy.*
But are there cares and business with the pleasure?
       Echo. *Leisure.*
Light, joy, and leisure; but shall they persever?
       Echo. *Ever.*

The following extract is from a seventeenth century poem about the rivalry between Cavaliers and Roundheads, and is attributed to Abraham Cowley.

> **2.** Now Echo on what's religion grounded?
> *Round-head.*
> Whose its professor most considerable?
> *Rabble.*
> How do these prove themselves to be godly?
> *Oddly.*
> But they in life are known to be the holy?
> *O lie.*

*ELEGIAC STANZA (see quatrain – heroic)

END-STOPPED LINE
An end-stopped line is one which finishes on a natural pause, either at the end of a phrase, clause or sentence. The meaning of the words is contained within the **metre** of the line. There is often some form of punctuation (comma, semi-colon, colon or full stop etc.) at the end of the line, but this is not always necessary. Most eighteenth century verse made use of the end-stopped line.

Examples:

1. From *An Essay on Criticism* by Alexander Pope

A little learning is a dangerous thing;
Drink deep, or taste not the Pierian spring:
There shallow draughts intoxicate the brain,
And drinking largely sobers us again.

2. From *Weathers* by Thomas Hardy

This is the weather the cuckoo likes,
    And so do I;
When showers betumble the chestnut spikes,
    And nestlings fly:
And the little brown nightingale bills his best,
And they sit outside at 'The Travellers' Rest',
And maids come forth sprig-muslin drest,
And citizens dream of the south and west,
    And so do I.

*ENGLYN
The englyn is a Welsh or Celtic form of poem based on both syllables and rhyme.

The Form

● Four lines (a **quatrain**) containing 30 syllables in all.

● The first line has ten syllables; the second line has six syllables and the third and fourth lines have seven syllables (10, 6, 7, 7).

● The sixth syllable of the first line introduces the rhyme, and the last syllable of the second, third and fourth lines rhyme with it. (The end of the first line does not rhyme.)

Examples:

1. A powdering of snow lies on the fields   10
And Spring is yet to show;   6
But somehow the wild geese know   7
They are being called to go.   7

        SB

2. The test of a good friend, they say, is this:
Neither borrow, nor lend;
And when you're at your wit's end
Know on whom you can depend.

        SB

*ENVOI
(also envoy) The word *envoi* comes from the French word meaning 'a sending on the way'. It is a final **stanza**, usually shorter in length, found in the **ballade, chant royal** and the **sestina**. In the ballade it is usually addressed to the poet's patron or to the subject of the poem. In the sestina it follows a particular pattern and consists of three lines which use the six repeated words in a set order.

(see entries for the relevant forms for examples)

EPIC VERSE

An epic is a long poem which tells the story of one or more heroes and warriors. It follows their adventures and exploits as they go through life confronting evil (sometimes supernatural) and overcoming the odds, often for the greater glory of a nation and its people. It mixes myth and legend with real history and tells its tale on a grand scale. Good examples of famous epic poems originating in the oral tradition are the *Iliad* (central hero is Achilles) and the *Odyssey* (central hero is Odysseus), both by Homer; the Anglo-Saxon epic *Beowulf*; and the Indian epics, the *Mahabharata* and the *Ramayana*. Of later poems in the epic mode, but which were written rather than oral in origin, perhaps some of the most well-known examples are Milton's *Paradise Lost*; Spenser's *The Faerie Queene*; Byron's *Don Juan*; and Tennyson's *Idylls of the King* (about King Arthur). Modern poets tend not to write epic poems as both the novel and the cinema have proved more satisfying media for artists to deal with such subjects.

EPIGRAM

An epigram is a short, witty and often satirical statement which can be in either verse or prose. Originally epigrams were designed as inscriptions for statues and monuments, but poets took them up as a genre in which they could express thoughts on people or life in a pithy and memorable way, with a graceful turn of phrase.

The following examples are all **couplet**s, although an epigram may be longer.

1. *Epigram on Singers* by Samuel Taylor Coleridge
Swans sing before they die – 'twere no bad thing
Should certain persons die before they sing.

2. *Epigram on Wit* by Alexander Pope
You beat your pate, and fancy wit will come;
Knock as you please, there's nobody at home!

3. *Marriage* by William Blake
When a man has married a wife he finds out whether
Her knees and elbows are only glued together.

EPITAPH
An epitaph was originally a verse inscription on a grave or tombstone. In more recent times, epitaphs have also appeared in print. An epitaph may praise the dead person in a solemn tone, or it may comment on the life or death of the person in a satirical or humorous manner. Several well-known epitaphs use puns in referring to the manner of life or death of the subject.

Examples:

1. *From the tomb of Thomas Gooding in Norwich Cathedral*
Thomas Gooding here do Staye
Wayting for God's Judgement Daye

All you that do this place pass bye
Remember death for you must dye
   As you are now even so was I
   And as I am so shall you be

2. *An Epitaph at Great Torrington, Devon*
Here lies a man who was killed by lightning;
He died when his prospects seemed to be brightening.
He might have cut a flash in this world of trouble,
But the flash cut him, and he lies in the stubble.

3. *Epitaph from Aberdeen*
Here lie the bones of Elizabeth Charlotte
Born a virgin, died a harlot
She was aye a virgin at seventeen
A remarkable thing in Aberdeen.

4. *Epitaph for a Dentist*
Stranger! Approach this spot with gravity!
John Brown is filling his last cavity.

FREE VERSE
Free verse (also known as *vers libre*) is poetry which has no regular line-length or metre. Its rhythms come from natural speech patterns, though the language may be heightened, and it can be very effective when used by poets who understand and have a feeling for the music and rhythms of more formal verse. In the hands of less able writers it can be a hit or miss affair. The term is often misapplied to writing by people who either cannot be

bothered to apply themselves to the craft, do not know anything about poetry or prefer to 'let it all hang out'. Free verse is not just prose chopped up into lines.

It has been a popular technique in the twentieth century and has been used by, among others, D. H. Lawrence, T. S. Eliot, Ezra Pound and William Carlos Williams.

However, in earlier times much of the King James translation of the Bible (The Authorised Version) was in, what today we might call, free verse, and several nineteenth century poets experimented along free verse lines, namely William Blake, Gerard Manley Hopkins and particularly, the American poet, Walt Whitman.

Example:

When I Peruse the Conquer'd Fame by Walt Whitman

When I peruse the conquer'd fame of heroes and the victories of
    mighty generals, I do not envy the generals,
Nor the President in his Presidency, nor the rich in his great
    house,
But when I hear of the brotherhood of lovers, how it was with
    them,
How together through life, through dangers, odium, unchanging,
    long and long,
Through youth and through middle and old age, how
    unfaltering, how affectionate and faithful they were,
Then I am pensive – I hastily walk away fill'd with the bitterest
    envy.

*HAIKU (pronounced HIGH-koo; the plural is also *haiku*) Haiku is a Japanese form. It has no particular rhyme or metre but is a short poem based on a set number of syllables. In the Japanese examples subjects are usually taken from the natural world, but since the form was adopted by western writers, this has widened to include any subject the poet wishes to write about.

The Form

- There are three short lines only, containing 17 syllables in all.

- There are five in the first line, seven in the second, and five in the third line (5, 7, 5).

Since it is so short, the haiku is often described as being like a stone dropped in a pool. The initial impact of the poem on the reader is like the impact of the stone on the water. The ripples the poem creates resonate in the mind for some time afterwards. So, after its first impression, a haiku should leave you thinking about its images and insights into life. Good haiku are hard to write but it can be very rewarding to sum up a truth in so few words. Although short, they often take longer to perfect than other, seemingly more complicated, poems.

Examples:

1. Owl haunts like a wraith   5
   While the hedgerow holds its breath.   7
   Death is on the wing.   5

                                                   SB

2. The queen of the hive
   Cannot fly free; she mothers
   A whole dynasty.

                                          SB

. . . .

*HEROIC COUPLET An heroic couplet is two rhyming lines of **iambic pentameter**. It was one of the most common metrical forms in English poetry until the nineteenth century and was first used by Geoffrey Chaucer, notably in *The Canterbury Tales*. Whole **stanza**s may be written in heroic couplets, or the couplets may be free-standing. If each line completes a grammatical phrase with the second line of the couplet ending a unit of meaning, it is called a closed heroic couplet.

(see also **quatrain – heroic**)

The first poem is an example of heroic couplets, while the second poem shows the use of closed heroic couplets.

Examples:

1. *Abou Ben Adhem* by James Leigh Hunt

Abou Ben Adhem (may his tribe increase!)
Awoke one night from a deep dream of peace,
And saw, within the moonlight in his room,
Making it rich, and like a lily in bloom,
An angel writing in a book of gold: –
Exceeding peace had made Ben Adhem bold,
And to the presence in the room he said,
'What writest thou?' – The vision raised its head,
And with a look made all of sweet accord,
Answered, 'The names of those who love the Lord.'
'And is mine one?' said Abou. 'Nay, not so,'
Replied the angel. Abou spoke more low,
But cheerly still; and said, 'I pray thee, then,
Write me as one who loves his fellow men.'
The angel wrote, and vanished. The next night
It came again with a great wakening light,
And showed the names whom love of God had blest,
And lo! Ben Adhem's name led all the rest.

2. From *Peter Grimes* by George Crabbe

Thus by himself compelled to live each day,
To wait for certain hours the tide's delay;
At the same times the same dull views to see,
The bounding marsh-bank and the blighted tree;
The water only, when the tides were high,
When low, the mud half-covered and half-dry;
The sun-burnt tar that blisters on the planks,
And bank-side stakes in their uneven ranks;
Heaps of entangled weeds that slowly float,
As the tide rolls by the impeded boat.

*KYRIELLE (pronounced KI-ri-EL) A kyrielle takes its name from a prayer in the church liturgy, the *Kyrie eleison*, from the Greek, meaning *Lord, have pity*. The main characteristic of this prayer is the frequent repetitions of the phrase, *kyrie eleison*. The kyrielle, therefore, is a verse form, originating in the French medieval period, which has a word, phrase or whole line repeated throughout the poem. Many hymns use this form but a kyrielle is not exclusively for religious verse.

The Form

● Each line has eight syllables, usually written in **iamb**ic **tetrameter**.

● It can be written in **couplet**s when it rhymes a, **A**, a, **A** throughout (**A** being the repeated line or word).

● Or it can also be written in **quatrain**s, rhyming a, a, b, **B**, c, c, b, **B** etc. or a, b, a, **B** c, b, c, **B** etc.

Example:

Kyrielle by SB

Dead leaves are on the steps again,	a
I tread on their fragility.	b
Another year clogs up the drain.	a
O, God of silence, let me be.	**B**

An owl is hooting in the Square –
The voice of our mortality.
The church is closed and no one's there.
O, God of silence, let me be.

There is a grave some miles from here,
A double home for family;
Dead leaves the only souvenir.
O, God of silence, let me be.

Don't tread upon the dead leaves of
The child I was, who's still with me.
Wind and time will make their move.
O, God of silence, let me be.

LAY An old French form of lyric poem which was composed to be sung by minstrels. Lays either told of love, or were stories of adventure and romance. Some, for example, dealt with tales from the Arthurian legends. The term has also been applied to verse in English which could be said to be a song-like narrative, such as Lord Macaulay's *Lays of Ancient Rome*.

LIGHT VERSE
Light verse is a general term for poetry which is not principally serious, although it may have a serious point to make behind its more frivolous façade. Light verse includes such forms as **limericks**, **epigrams**, **epitaphs**, **nonsense verse**, **clerihews**, **ruthless rhymes**, **satire** and **parody**. The best light verse is often written with a light touch and wit, and is usually entertaining in nature. Much of it is anonymous but some good examples of masters of light verse would be Lewis Carroll, W. S. Gilbert, Hilaire Belloc, Ogden Nash, John Betjeman, Wendy Cope, and Gavin Ewart.

*LIMERICK
A limerick is a short form of **light verse** predominantly in **anapæst**ic metre. It is almost always humorous, and often quite scurrilous, in content. To be really successful it requires wit and wordplay; usually the least successful are those which are simply too tame or too blatantly obvious in their sexual language.

The Form

- Five lines, rhyming a, a, b, b, a.

- Lines 1, 2 and 5 have three **feet** – usually either one **iamb** and two anapæsts or sometimes three anapæsts.

- Lines 3 and 4 have two feet usually either two anapæsts or one iamb and one anapæst.

- Most limericks have first lines which end with the place of origin of the subject of the rhyme.

Examples:

1. There was a young lady of Trent,
Who said that she knew what it meant
When men asked her to dine
With cocktails and wine,
She knew what it meant – but she went.
                                        Anon

2. A wanton young lady of Wimley
  Reproached for not acting primly,
  Answered: 'Heavens above!
  I know sex isn't love,
  But it's such an attractive facsimile.'

Anon

Edward Lear is probably the most famous writer of limericks. Many of his limericks followed a pattern of repeating a large part of the first line again in the last, though not all do this.

Examples:

3. There was an Old Person of Bray,
  Who sang through the whole of the Day
  To his Ducks and his Pigs,
  Whom he fed upon Figs,
  That valuable Person of Bray.

Edward Lear

4. There was a young lady of Wilts,
  Who walked up to Scotland on stilts;
  When they said it was shocking
  To show so much stocking,
  She answered, "Then what about kilts?"

Edward Lear

The limerick lends itself to being parodied and played with in several ingenious ways.

Examples:

5. There was an old man of St Bees
  Who was horribly stung by a wasp.
  When they said: 'Does it hurt?'
  He replied: 'No, it doesn't –
  It's a good job it wasn't a hornet!'

W. S. Gilbert

6. A man hired by John Smith and Co.
  Loudly declared he would tho.
  Man that he saw
  Dumping dirt by his store.
  The drivers, therefore, didn't do.

Mark Twain

The Semantic Limerick

The semantic limerick was invented, as far as I know, by the twentieth century poet, Gavin Ewart. It consists of rewriting a well-known limerick without using the actual words in the original. Instead the poet must find other ways of saying the same thing by using definitions from the dictionary for the replaced words. The following is one of his best examples.

The Semantic Limerick According to the Shorter Oxford English Dictionary (1933)

There existed an adult male person who had lived a relatively short time, belonging or pertaining to St John's,* who desired to commit sodomy with the large web-footed swimming birds of the genus *Cygnus* or subfamily *Cygninae* of the family *Anatidae*, characterized by a long and gracefully curved neck and a majestic motion when swimming.

So he moved into the presence of the person employed to carry burdens, who declared: 'Hold or possess as something at your disposal my female child! The large web-footed swimming-birds of the genus *Cygnus* or subfamily *Cygninae* of the family *Anatidae*, characterized by a long and gracefully curved neck and a majestic motion when swimming, are set apart, specially retained for the Head, Fellows and Tutors of the College!'

*A College of Cambridge University

Gavin Ewart

The original is as follows, for comparison:

> There was a young student of John's,
> Who wanted to b*gg*r some swans.
> But the loyal hall-porter
> Said: 'Please take my daughter,
> For the swans are reserved for the Dons.'

Anon

*LITTLE WILLIE The Little Willie is a modern name for the sort of rhymes made famous by Harry Graham, and known as **ruthless rhymes**. These tell of somebody who usually meets a very macabre ending and are told in a jaunty **metre** and a very matter of fact way. This is where the humour lies and these poems definitely belong in the light verse area, in spite of their gruesome subject matter. Although taking its name from Little Willie, this form has expanded to include any member of the family.

The Form

- Four lines – a **quatrain** usually rhyming a, b, a, b or a, a, b, b. This sometimes expands to two **stanza**s.

- Each line has four feet or a **tetrameter**, often in **trochaic** metre.

- The subject of the rhyme is either Little Willie, or another member of the family.

- The content of the rhyme is invariably of someone meeting a grisly end.

Examples:

1. Little Willie from his mirror
Licked the mercury right off
Thinking, in his childish error,
It would cure the whooping cough.

At the funeral his mother
Brightly said to Mrs Brown:
'Twas a chilly day for Willie
When the mercury went down!'
Anon

2. Billy, in one of his nice new sashes,
Fell in the fire and was burned to ashes;
Now, although the room grows chilly,
I haven't the heart to poke poor Billy.
Harry Graham

3. Late last night I slew my wife
Stretched her on the parquet flooring.
I was loath to take her life,
But I had to stop her snoring.
Harry Graham

LYRIC POETRY
A lyric was originally a song and is, in this sense, still used in music today. In poetry, a lyric is a reasonably short poem which usually expresses the thoughts and emotions of a single speaker, which may be the poet himself or herself, or may be a persona adopted by the writer. There is a romantic air about lyric poetry and many love poems, as well as religious verse, can be said to be lyrical. Lyric poetry can be in any form, and there are so many examples of lyric verse that the following have been chosen quite at random.

Examples:

1. *Upon Julia's Voice* by Robert Herrick
So smooth, so sweet, so silvery, is thy voice
As, could they hear, the damned would make no noise,
But listen to thee (walking in thy chamber)
Melting melodious words to lutes of amber.

2. *The Bargain* (a sonnet) by Sir Philip Sidney
My true love hath my heart, and I have his,
By just exchange, one for the other given.
I hold his dear, and mine he cannot miss,
There never was a better bargain driven.
His heart in me keeps me and him in one,
My heart in him his thoughts and senses guides;
He loves my heart, for once it was his own,
I cherish his, because in me it bides.
His heart his wound receivèd from my sight,
My heart was wounded with his wounded heart;
For as from me on him his hurt did light,
So still methought in me his hurt did smart.
Both equal hurt, in this change sought our bliss:
My true love hath my heart and I have his.

3. *Fair Isle at Sea – thy lovely name* by Robert Louis Stevenson
Fair Isle at Sea – thy lovely name
Soft in my ear like music came.
That sea I loved, and once or twice
I touched at isles of Paradise.

METAPHOR Metaphor is a figure of speech related to the **simile**.

However, whereas a simile uses the words *like* or *as* in comparing two different things, a metaphor dispenses with these 'bridge' words and basically says that one thing *is* the other. A metaphor shows a similarity between two completely different things by describing the one in terms of the other.

Metaphor is used in everyday speech all the time, as in expressions such as 'He was born with two left feet', 'He's a sly old fox', and 'To have your cake and eat it too'.

In such uses the literal meaning of the words is not their real meaning. The more colourful language of the metaphor serves to describe something else.

Metaphors such as 'the foot of the stairs' or 'the arm of the chair' have become so much a part of the language that they are called *dead metaphors* – they no longer have a life that could be considered metaphorical.

Metaphor is, however, at the very heart of poetry and it is a poet's job to see connections and similarities which can be used to explain things vividly and make them memorable. Shakespeare's 'Seven Ages of Man' from *As You Like It* is probably one of the best known metaphors in poetry, comparing, as it does, man's life to an actor playing many different parts as he grows older ('All the world's a stage ...') and one of the most famous twentieth century extended metaphor poems is Stevie Smith's *Not Waving But Drowning*. Poets normally, however, employ metaphor within the poem, sometimes in just a word or a phrase.

The metaphors in the first example are all highlighted in italics.

Examples:

1. From *The Darkling Thrush* by Thomas Hardy

I leant upon a coppice gate
When Frost was spectre-gray,
And Winter's *dregs* made desolate
The weakening *eye* of day.
The tangled bine-stems *scored* the sky
Like strings of broken lyres,

And all mankind that haunted nigh
Had sought their household fires.

The land's sharp features seemed to be
The Century's *corpse* outleant,
His crypt the cloudy canopy,
The wind his death-lament,
The ancient *pulse* of germ and birth
Was shrunken hard and dry,
And every spirit upon earth
Seemed fervourless as I.

The theme of the following poem is the idea of the road as a metaphor for life and death.

2. *Uphill* by Christina Rossetti

Does the road wind uphill all the way?
Yes, to the very end.
Will the day's journey take the whole long day?
From morn to night, my friend.

But is there for the night a resting-place?
A roof for when the slow, dark hours begin.
May not the darkness hide it from my face?
You cannot miss that inn.

Shall I meet other wayfarers at night?
Those who have gone before.
Then must I knock, or call when just in sight?
They will not keep you standing at the door.

Shall I find comfort, travel-sore and weak?
Of labour you shall find the sum.
Will there be beds for me and all who seek?
Yea, beds for all who come.

* * *

*MINUTE The minute is a recent form invented by an American called Verna Lee Hine Gardner. It is based on the number of seconds in a minute.

The Form

● It has 60 syllables in total.

- The syllables are spread over 12 lines as follows: 8 syllables in the first, fifth and ninth lines and 4 syllables in all other lines.

- It is written in **iambic rhythm** (di-dum).

- It is punctuated as prose, in that capital letters only appear after full stops and not necessarily at the beginnings of lines.

- It rhymes in **couplets** a,a, b,b, c,c, d,d, e,e, f,f.

Example:

In a Minute by SB

One minute isn't very long	8
to sing a song,	4
to cook a meal,	4
or change a wheel.	4
A minute really is too short,	8
I would have thought,	4
to make a friend,	4
or buck the trend.	4
And yet it's clearly long enough	8
to cut up rough,	4
to bomb Japan,	4
to kill a man.	4

*NAGA-UTA This is a Japanese form, meaning 'long song', which is based on a set number of syllables per line. As it is longer than other well-known Japanese forms, such as **haiku** and **tanka**, it offers more scope for a writer and is suited to more lyrical verse. These forms generally rely entirely on syllables and do not employ rhyme or specific rhythms. However, western writers who have adopted some of these forms occasionally add rhythm and rhyme in places. The western tradition of poetry is based on rhythm and rhyme and this comes more naturally. Purists dislike this tendency, but all forms should be open to adaptation and play, once a writer has mastered them in their original.

The Form

- The first line has 5 syllables and the second has 7 syllables.

This pattern is repeated throughout the poem which can be as long as the writer wishes.

● The poem finishes with an extra line of 7 syllables.

NONSENSE VERSE
Nonsense poetry is really an invention of English verse. The peculiar trait of seeing the absurd and funny side of man's existence, the ability to laugh at the serious things of life and to exploit their incongruity, is an important element of English humour. Nonsense verse as a *genre* could be said to have begun in the nineteenth century with Lewis Carroll and Edward Lear. There have always existed what might be called nonsense rhymes; for example, many nursery rhymes show the wordplay and humour of nonsense. However, it was Lear and Carroll who raised its status and led the way for many writers since: Hilaire Belloc, Stevie Smith, Spike Milligan and, of course, Anon(!), to name but a few who have successfully explored the genre. The term came into common use after Edward Lear published *A Book of Nonsense* in 1846. Among his best-known nonsense poems are *The Owl and the Pussycat*, *The Jumblies*, *The Pobble who has no Toes* and *The Dong with the Luminous Nose*.

Nonsense verse has a kind of illogical logic of its own. At first reading it seems not to make any real sense, and yet it also *does* appear to be saying something. Such contradictions intrigue and delight if the verse is well-written. Rhyme and strong rhythm are usually important in nonsense verse, and the humour arises more from the topsy-turvy world being described than from any mainstream jokes.

Lewis Carroll was a gifted mathematician who lectured at Oxford and knew all about logic and reason. He was also a gifted writer, with a strong sense of the absurd. In his masterpieces, *Alice's Adventures in Wonderland* and *Through the Looking-Glass*, he turned logic on its head and created a surreal world which seemed to operate on its own alternative or parallel logic. This is the world we may experience in dreams, but the writer of nonsense verse can control what happens, even using the genre for **satire** and **parody** as Lewis Carroll certainly did. Among his best-known nonsense poems are *Jabberwocky*, *The Hunting of the Snark*, *Humpty Dumpty's*

Recitation and *The White Knight's Ballad*, all of which have a peculiar logic of their own.

Examples:

1. *Nursery Rhyme* Anon

I dreamed a dream next Tuesday week,
Beneath the apple-trees;
I thought my eyes were big pork-pies,
And my nose was Stilton cheese.
The clock struck twenty minutes to six,
When a frog sat on my knee;
I asked him to lend me eighteenpence,
But he borrowed a shilling of me.

2. *Cold are the Crabs* by Edward Lear

Cold are the crabs that crawl on yonder hills,
Colder the cucumbers that grow beneath,
And colder still the brazen chops that wreathe
    The tedious gloom of philosophic pills!
For when the tardy film of nectar fills
The ample bowls of demons and of men,
There lurks the feeble mouse, the homely hen,
    And there the porcupine with all her quills.
Yet much remains – to weave a solemn strain
That lingering sadly – slowly dies away,
Daily departing with departing day
A pea green gamut on a distant plain
When wily walruses in congress meet –
    Such such is life —

3. *Evidence read at the Trial of the Knave of Hearts* by Lewis Carroll

They told me you had been to her,
And mentioned me to him:
She gave me a good character,
But said I could not swim.

He sent them word I had not gone,
(We know it to be true):
If she should push the matter on,
What would become of you?

I gave her one, they gave him two,
You gave us three or more;
They all returned from him to you,
Though they were mine before.

If I or she should chance to be
Involved in this affair,
He trusts to you to set them free,
Exactly as they were.

My notion was that you had been
(Before she had this fit)
An obstacle that came between
Him and ourselves, and it.

Don't let him know she liked them best,
For this must ever be
A secret kept from all the rest,
Between yourself and me.

OCTAVE

OCTAVE An octave is a group of eight lines, also known as an **octet**. If these eight lines make up a **stanza** it is usually **ottava rima**, but can also just refer to any eight-line **stanza**. Otherwise, an octave refers specifically to the first eight lines of a Petrarchan **sonnet**.

OCTET

OCTET (see octave)

*ODE

*ODE An ode is a lyric poem, usually quite long, which is formal and lofty in tone and deals with grand and serious subjects. There are two types of ode – the poem written for public celebration of great figures or events, and the one which is a more private meditation, exploring more personal thoughts and emotions. Both kinds could be said to be poems of praise.

The ode takes its name from a Greek word meaning 'song', and the generally accepted originator of the form was the Greek poet, Pindar (fifth century BC). Pindaric odes were choral songs written for public occasions, often to celebrate success in the Olympic Games. They consisted of a set pattern of **stanzas** based on the chorus in Greek drama.

The other main type of ode is known as the Horatian ode, after the Latin poet, Horace (first century BC). These belong to the more personal sphere of writing and each stanza of an Horatian ode follows the metrical pattern of the first stanza.

Many English poets have experimented with the ode and set their own patterns, or even dispensed with regular metre or rhyme altogether. Odes (Pindaric or Homeric) without any regular pattern of rhyme, metre or stanza length are known as irregular odes. (A good example is William Wordsworth's *Ode: Intimations of Immortality*.) What unifies all the different variations is a certain grandeur of style and an air of praise and celebration in the treatment of subjects. Today the ode is rarely written as its very formality and high-flown language do not seem to suit our modern times. In the twentieth century the ode was often subverted as a form for comic purposes, and the few recent odes tend to be satirical or humorous in tone.

Keats' Form

John Keats invented the following pattern for his famous poem, *Ode to a Nightingale*.

- This form is in the tradition of the Horation ode.
- Each stanza has ten lines, and there are eight stanzas in all.
- Each stanza is written basically in **iamb**ic **pentameter**, except for the eighth line which is in iambic **trimeter**.
- The stanza rhyme scheme is: a, b, a, b, c, d, e, c, d, e.

From *Ode to a Nightingale* by John Keats

My heart aches, and a drowsy numbness pains
    My sense, as though of hemlock I had drunk,
Or emptied some dull opiate to the drains
    One minute past, and Lethe-wards had sunk:
'Tis not through envy of thy happy lot,
    But being too happy in thy happiness,
That thou, light-wingèd Dryad of the trees,
        In some melodious plot
Of beechen green, and shadows numberless,
    Singest of summer in full throated ease.

Shelley's Form

Shelley invented the following pattern for his famous poem, *Ode to a Skylark*.

- This form is also in the tradition of the Horatian ode.

- Each stanza has five lines, and there are 21 stanzas in all.

- Each stanza is written basically in **trochaic trimeter** (dum-di, dum-di, dum-di) except for the last line which is basically in **iambic hexameter**, or **alexandrine** metre.

- The rhyme scheme for each stanza is a, b, a, b, b.

From *Ode to a Skylark* by Percy Bysshe Shelley

Hail to thee, blithe spirit!
  Bird thou never wert –
That from heaven or near it
  Pourest thy full heart
In profuse strains of unpremeditated art.

Higher still and higher
  From the earth thou springest,
Like a cloud of fire;
  The blue deep thou wingest,
And singing still dost soar, and soaring ever singest.

OTTAVA RIMA Ottava rima is a stanza of eight lines, written in **iambic pentameter**. It was originally an Italian form which was introduced into English verse in the sixteenth century by Sir Thomas Wyatt. It has not been greatly used in English, although the Romantic poets, Keats and Shelley, and most notably Byron, revived it. Byron's long, narrative, satirical poem, *Don Juan*, is written completely in ottava rima, and the form is ideally suited to the subject matter and conversational tone of this *tour de force*. Occasionally other poets have returned to ottava rima, and a fine, more modern example is W.B.Yeats' poem, *Sailing to Byzantium*.

The Form

- Each stanza has eight lines.

- Each line is an iambic pentameter (di-dum, di-dum, di-dum, di-dum, di-dum), although, as with any strict metre, there are occasional variations within the five-stress line.

- Each stanza rhymes as follows: a, b, a, b, a, b, c, c.

Example:

From *Don Juan* by Lord Byron

Most epic poets plunge in *media res*
(Horace makes this the heroic turnpike road),
And then your hero tells whene'er you please
What went before by way of episode,
While seated after dinner at his ease
Beside his mistress in some soft abode,
Palace or garden, paradise or cavern,
Which serves the happy couple for a tavern.

That is the usual method, but not mine;
My way is to begin at the beginning.
The regularity of my design
Forbids all wandering as the worst of sinning,
And therefore I shall open with a line
(Although it cost me half an hour in spinning)
Narrating somewhat of Don Juan's father
And also of his mother, if you'd rather.

. . .

A little curly-headed, good-for-nothing,
And mischief-making monkey from his birth;
His parents ne'er agreed except in doting
Upon the most unquiet imp on earth.
Instead of quarrelling, had they been but both in
Their senses, they'd have sent young master forth
To school or had him soundly whipped at home
To teach him manners for the time to come.

*PANTOUM (also pantun) The pantoum is a verse form which originates from Malayan and other South-East Asian literature. It was introduced to western writers in the nineteenth century and has been most used by French poets, although some English writers have experimented with it.

The form is based on a set pattern of repeated lines and is most suited to subject matter which describes an atmosphere; continuous, but slow moving, events; or thoughts and emotions on a theme. The repeated lines can offer opportunities for different nuances of meaning by varying the punctuation, but they do not easily allow for a story to move along very fast!

The Form

● Each stanza is a **quatrain** (four lines) and there can be any number of stanzas.

● Each stanza rhymes as follows: a, b, a, b   b, c, b, c etc. and can be in any regular **metre**.

● The stanzas are interlinked as follows: the second and fourth lines of each stanza become the first and third of the next. In the last stanza the third and first lines of the very first stanza become the second and fourth, so that the poem ends with the same line as it began.

Example:

Foot and Mouth by SB

Where once the fields were living, breathing places,
Now all that's left to shoot at are the crows;
Where once we looked out on a field of faces,
Now there's the silence everybody knows,

Now all that's left to shoot at are the crows.
No more the motley choir of bleating sheep,
Now, there's the silence everybody knows –
Dear God, the very fields seem asleep.

No more the motley choir of bleating sheep –
Only the wind shudders on the hill;
Dear God, the very fields seem asleep
And all that mighty heart is lying still.

Only the wind shudders on the hill,
Only the dust shivers on the farm,
And all that mighty heart is lying still –
After the storm, the long unnatural calm.

Only the dust shivers on the farm
Where once we looked out on a field of faces;
After the storm, the long unnatural calm
Where once the fields were living, breathing places.

PARODY
Parody is an imitation of another writer's style, ideas, or of a specific piece of work. It makes fun of the original, treating often serious or portentous works with flippancy and sometimes, spite. Parody is a subversive genre written with a caustic wit to cut the subject down to size. Lewis Carroll, in his *Alice* books, parodied many famous Victorian poems which children of the day were forced to learn for their moral improvement. His parodies appealed to his readers not only because of their humour, but also because they deliberately did *not* contain a moral. Interestingly, many of Carroll's parodies are now better known than the originals upon which they were based. Parody could be said to be a branch of **satire**.

Examples:

1. See Christina Rossetti's poem, *A Birthday*, in the entry on **simile**, for the original of this parody.

My heart is like one asked to dine
Whose evening dress is up the spout;
My heart is like a man would be
Whose raging tooth is half pulled out.
My heart is like a howling swell
Who boggles on his upper C;
My heart is madder than all these –
My wife's mamma has come to tea.

Raise me a bump upon my crown,
Bang it till green in purple dies;
Feed me on bombs and fulminates,
And turncocks of a medium size.
Work me a suit in crimson apes
And sky-blue beetles on the spree;
Because the mother of my wife
Has come – and means to stay with me.

Anon

2. The following is Lewis Carroll's parody of a well-known Isaac Watts' poem whose moral lesson begins, 'How doth the little busy bee / Improve the shining hour . . . .'

How doth the little crocodile
Improve his shining tail,
And pour the waters of the Nile
On every golden scale!

How cheerfully he seems to grin,
How neatly spreads his claws,
And welcomes little fishes in
With gently smiling jaws!

3. The following is the opening of Lewis Carroll's parody of a popular song of the time from the opera, *The Bohemian Girl*, (1843) which begins, 'I dreamt that I dwelt in marble halls . . . .'

The Palace of Humbug

I dreamt I dwelt in marble halls,
And each damp thing that creeps and crawls
Went wobble-wobble on the walls.

Faint odours of departed cheese,
Blown on the dank unwholesome breeze,
Awoke the never-ending sneeze.

Strange pictures decked the arras drear,
Strange characters of woe and fear,
The humbugs of the social sphere.

One showed a vain and noisy prig,
That shouted empty words and big
At him that nodded in a wig.

· ·

QUATRAIN
A quatrain is a **stanza** of four lines, either rhymed or unrhymed, which can occur in any **metre**. It is the most common stanza length in English poetry, and where rhyme is used the most popular rhyme schemes are as follows: 1. a, b, a, b; 2. a, a, b, b; 3. a, b, b, a; 4. a, b, –, b 5. –, a, –, a and 6. a, a, a, a.

*The Heroic Quatrain

The heroic quatrain is also known as the **elegiac stanza**. This is written in **iambic pentameter**, rhyming a, b, a, b (see also **heroic couplet**).

Example:

> From *Elegy written in a Country Churchyard* by Thomas Gray
> The Curfew tolls the knell of parting day,
> The lowing herd wind slowly o'er the lea,
> The plowman homeward plods his weary way,
> And leaves the world to darkness and to me.

(see also **ballad**, **rubai** and **sapphic verse**)

QUINTAIN (also known as quintet) This is any **stanza** of five lines. The quintet is specifically a five-line rhyming stanza. The rhyme scheme as well as the metre of each line, may vary. A common rhyme scheme is a, b, a, b, b, but many other schemes are possible.

(see also **cinquain**)

REFRAIN A refrain is a repeated word, phrase, line (or lines) which occurs at intervals throughout the poem, usually at the ends of stanzas. It is particularly used in several of the strict forms of verse, such as the **ballad**, **ballade**, **kyrielle**, **rondeau**, **rondel**, **rondelet**, **roundel**, **triolet** and **villanelle**. It may also serve as a chorus in a poem or rhyme of the sort used in both folk and popular songs to encourage people to join in.

*RENGA Renga is a traditional Japanese form based on syllables and is a series of linked **haiku** which act as stanzas in the longer poem. A renga is a communal effort and is written by a number of people. Each person takes it in turn to add a haiku, taking as its theme something suggested or touched on by the previous one. In the final haiku the writer tries to draw together the threads of all the previous ones to bring the renga to some sort of conclusion. It has not been a particularly popular or used form in English but can repay some experimentation, and it is especially useful as an exercise for writing groups. When attempting renga for the first time it could help if the group chooses an overall theme before starting, such as *time, summer, growing older, love* or *death*.

The Form

- It is a series of haiku written by two or more different people in turn.

- Each stanza is a haiku with three lines containing five, seven and five syllables respectively.

- Each succeeding haiku takes its theme from the previous haiku.

- The final haiku rounds off the whole poem.

- There is no limit to the number of haiku that can be used in the poem.

*RHYME ROYAL

Rhyme royal is a **stanza** form of seven lines. It is thought to have acquired its name from King James I of Scotland who used it for his long poem, *Kingis Quair* or The King's Book, written while he was imprisoned by the English at the beginning of the fifteenth century. However, this stanza form had been used by writers before him, notably by Geoffrey Chaucer, and it is also known as the Chaucerian stanza. Examples of Chaucer's use of rhyme royal can be found in the *Clerk's Tale* from *The Canterbury Tales*, *Troilus and Criseyde*, and the *Parlement of Foules*. Although it has been principally used as a stanza form by medieval and Elizabethan writers, it is quite suited to English verse and is, perhaps, due for a renaissance amongst those writers who enjoy experimenting with form.

The Form

- A stanza form of seven lines (a heptastich or **septet**) written in **iamb**ic **pentameter**.

- The rhyme scheme is as follows: a, b, a, b, b, c, c.

Examples:

1. From *Troilus and Criseyde* by Geoffrey Chaucer

This Troilus sat on his bayè steed,
All armèd, save his head, full richèly,
And wounded was his horse, and gan to bleed,
On which he rode a pace, full softèly;
But such a knightly sightè, truèly,
As was on him, was nought, withouten failè,
To look on Mars, that god is of battailè.

2. *An Epitaph* by Stephen Hawes (died 1523)

O mortal folk, you may behold and see
How I lie here, sometime a mighty knight;
The end of joy and all prosperitee
Is death at last, thorough his course and might:
After the day there cometh the dark night,
For though the daye be never so long,
At last the bells ringeth to evensong.

- -

*RIDDLE The riddle is an ancient literary device in which something is described, usually in the form of a question or puzzle, and listeners or readers have to guess what it is. One of the most famous and oldest of riddles is the riddle of the Sphinx as asked of Oedipus: 'What creature is that which moves on four feet in the morning, on two feet at noon-day, and on three towards the going down of the sun?' The answer is *Man*, who crawls on all fours as a child, walks upright as an adult, and walks with a stick when an old man. The riddle was a very popular form with the Anglo-Saxons and during the Middle Ages. The earliest recorded English riddles can be found in the *Exeter Book* which was written during the tenth century AD. However, riddles have remained popular to this day, and for poets, the third sort of riddle (listed below) offers plenty of scope for imaginative writing and use of **metaphor**.

There are three kinds of riddles. The first is the sort found in joke books and often using puns, such as, 'What's the difference between a ship's siren and a cowboy?' Answer: 'One hoots from the ship and the other shoots from the hip' and 'What's black and white and red (read) all over?' Answer: 'A newspaper'.

The second hides the answer in rhyming verse and is most often found in children's books. Such riddles spell out the answer, letter by letter, by clues given in each line containing pairs of linked words and usually sum up the whole in the last lines.

They usually run something like this:

> My first is in **c**harm but not in spell,
> My second's in he**a**ven but not in hell;
> My third's in my **t**ail and little pink **t**ongue,
> And many a poet my praises has sung.

The third sort is of more interest to a writer. These riddles are puzzles which describe the subject (or answer) but in such a way that it may not be immediately obvious. Use of **metaphor** and **simile** can help to conceal the answer although all that is said must be true. In order to solve such riddles a listener or reader must picture what is being described and use some divergent thinking to tease out the answer. Riddles of this kind are usually full of intriguing images and lyrical phrases, and are direct descendants of the Anglo-Saxon *Exeter Book* riddles. They often do not rhyme, but may do.

Examples:

1. From the *Exeter Book*, trans. Kevin Crossley-Holland
On the way a miracle: water became bone
Answer: Ice

2. In marble walls as white as milk,
Lined with a skin as soft as silk,
Within a fountain crystal clear
A golden apple doth appear.
No doors there are to this stronghold,
Yet thieves break in and steal the gold.
Answer: An Egg

Anon

*RONDEAU
The rondeau is an Old French lyric form containing a **refrain**. It was particularly popular among French writers in the sixteenth century but was not practised much in England until the nineteenth century when poets such as Swinburne, Dobson and Henley began to experiment with several of these old forms.

The Form

- It has 15 lines, two of which are the repeated one-line refrain. The refrain is usually the first phrase of the first line (but may only be one or two words).

- Each line has eight syllables (usually **tetrameter** or four feet). English poets often use ten syllables (usually **pentameter** or five feet).

- The lines are arranged in three **stanza**s of different length: the first has five lines, the second has four lines, and the third has six lines.

- There are only two rhyming sounds used throughout the poem.

- The rhyme scheme is as follows (**R** denotes the repeated refrain): the first stanza: a, a, b, b, a; the second stanza: a, a, b, **R** and the third stanza: a, a, b, b, a, **R**.

Example:

The Roman Road by Thomas Hardy

The Roman Road runs straight and bare	a
As the pale parting-line in hair	a
Across the heath. And thoughtful men	b
Contrast its days of Now and Then,	b
And delve, and measure, and compare;	a
Visioning on the vacant air	a
Helmed legionaries, who proudly rear	a
The Eagle, as they pace again	b
The Roman Road.	**R**
But no tall brass-helmed legionnaire	a
Haunts it for me. Uprises there	a
A mother's form upon my ken,	b
Guiding my infant steps, as when	b
We walked that ancient throroughfare,	a
The Roman Road.	**R**

The Ten-Line Rondeau

The ten-line rondeau is another form of rondeau whose structure is as follows.

The Form

● It has two stanzas each of which ends with a refrain.

● The refrain is just one word and this is the very first word of the poem.

● The first stanza has six lines (and the refrain), the second stanza has four lines (and the refrain).

● The rhyme scheme is: first stanza: a, b, b, a, a, b, **R** and the second stanza: a, b, b, a, **R.**

RONDEAU REDOUBLÉ
Rondeau redoublé is another of the French forms but is very rare. English poets have not really experimented with it at all as it is rather complex. Among French writers, La Fontaine was one of the few to try writing in this form. The details of rondeau redoublé are given below for interest, and in case there are writers who would like to test themselves against its demands!

The Form

● It has six **quatrain**s (four-line stanzas).

● Only two rhyming sounds are used (as in the **rondeau**).

● The rhyme scheme is as follows: first stanza: a, b, a, b; second stanza: b, a, b, a; third stanza; a, b, a, b; fourth stanza: b, a, b, a; fifth stanza: a, b, a, b and the sixth stanza: b, a, b, a, **R** (**R**: the refrain is the first half of the opening line).

● The four lines of the first stanza are used, in order, as the final lines of the second, third, fourth and fifth stanzas.

*RONDEL
The rondel is an Old French form, from the fourteenth century, using two **rhyme**s and a **refrain**, similar to the **rondeau**. It was written in English in the fifteenth century but, as with several other older forms, dropped out of fashion and was revived in the nineteenth century when poets such as Swinburne, Austin Dobson and W. E. Henley rediscovered them and enjoyed experimenting with them. There are a number of different variants

of the rondel, all of which are detailed below. However, the most common pattern is given first, along with an example.

The Form

- It has three **stanza**s.

- There is a two-line refrain (**A**, **B**) where the whole lines are repeated in each stanza.

- There are either 14 lines on the following rhyme scheme:
  A, B, b, a   a, b, **A, B**   a, b, b, a, **A, B.**

- Or there are 13 lines on the following rhyme scheme:
  A, B, b, a   a, b, **A, B**   a, b, b, a, *either* **A** or **B.**

Example:

We'll to the Woods by W. E. Henley

We'll to the woods and gather may	**A**
Fresh from the footprints of the rain.	**B**
We'll to the woods, at every vein	b
To drink the spirit of the day.	a
The winds of spring are out at play,	a
The needs of spring in heart and brain.	b
We'll to the woods and gather may	**A**
Fresh from the footprints of the rain.	**B**
The world's too near her end, you say?	a
Hark to the blackbird's mad refrain!	b
It waits for her, the vast Inane?	b
Then, girls, to help her on the way	a
We'll to the woods and gather may.	**A**

Swinburne experimented with the rondel and indeed, the form seems to be less fixed than others. Below is an example of one of Swinburne's rondels – it is written in **pentameter**s (with an **iamb**ic base), except for the last line of each stanza which is in **dimeter** and is the first phrase of the first line. It has only two stanzas. The 'c' rhyming sound is determined by the refrain (**R**).

Rondel by A. C. Swinburne

Kissing her hair I sat against her feet,	a
Wove and unwove it, wound and found it sweet;	a

Made fast therewith her hands, drew down her eyes,	b
Deep as deep flowers and dreamy like dim skies;	b
With her own tresses bound and found her fair,	c
Kissing her hair.	**R**

Sleep were no sweeter than her face to me,	d
Sleep of cold sea-bloom under the cold sea;	d
What pain could get between my face and hers?	e
What new sweet thing would love not relish worse?	e
Unless, perhaps, white death had kissed me there,	c
Kissing her hair?	**R**

Early Rondel Form

● It has eight lines, including repeated lines for the refrain.

● The rhyme scheme is: **A**, **B**, a, **A**, a, b, **A**, **B**.

Rondel Doublé (variation)

● It has 16 lines, including repeated lines for the refrain.

● The rhyme scheme is: **A**, **B**, **A**, **B**,   a, b, **B**, **A**,   a, b, b, a, **A**, **B**, **B**, **A**.

....

*RONDELET This form is a small version of the **rondel**, hence its name, rondelet.

The Form

● It has seven lines, including the repeated **refrain** (**A**) which is also the first line.

● The first, third and seventh lines are usually shorter and consist of two **iambic** feet.

● The second, fourth, fifth and sixth lines are usually written in iambic **tetrameter** (four feet).

● There are only two rhyming sounds and the scheme is as follows: **A**, b, **A**, a, b, b, **A**.

Example:

| Where are they now, | **A** |
| The ones I loved, who loved me too, | b |

Where are they now?   **A**
Buried so deep I can't allow   a
My mind to dwell on who was who   b
For fear of facing what is true.   b
Where are they now?   **A**

SB

---

*ROUNDEL

The roundel is another variation on the **rondeau** and **rondel**. However, it was invented in the nineteeth century by the English poet A. C. Swinburne.

The Form

● It has 11 lines, two of which are the **refrain** (**R**) which is the first phrase of the first line.

● All lines are **pentameter**s (five feet) except lines 4 and 11 (the refrains).

● There are three **stanza**s and only two rhyming sounds throughout.

● The rhyme scheme is as follows: first stanza: a, b, a, **R**; second stanza: b, a, b, a and the third stanza: a, b, a, **R**.

Example:

The Roundel by A. C. Swinburne

A roundel is wrought as a ring or a starbright sphere,   a
With craft of delight and with cunning of sound unsought,   b
That the heart of the hearer may smile if to pleasure his ear a
A roundel is wrought.   **R**

Its jewel of music is carven of all or of aught –   b
Love, laughter, or mourning – remembrance of rapture or fear – a
That fancy may fashion to hang in the ear of thought.   b

As a bird's quick song runs round, and the hearts in us hear a
Pause answer pause, and again the same strain caught,   b
So moves the device whence, round as a pearl or tear,   a
A roundel is wrought.   **R**

*RUBAI

The rubai is a verse form of four lines – a **quatrain**. (It takes its name from an Arabic word for quatrain.) A rubáiyát is a collection of quatrains, such as in the long poem, the *Rubáiyát of Omar Khayyám of Naishápúr* which was translated by the nineteenth century writer, Edward FitzGerald.

The Form

- Each **stanza** has four lines (FitzGerald wrote in **iambic pentameter**)

- The rhyme scheme is a, a, b, a.

Example:

From *Rubáiyát of Omar Khayyám of Naishápúr* trans. by Edward FitzGerald

The Moving Finger writes; and, having writ,	a
Moves on: nor all your Piety nor Wit	a
Shall lure it back to cancel half a Line,	b
Nor all your Tears wash out a Word of it.	a

And that inverted Bowl they call the Sky,
Whereunder crawling coop'd we live and die,
Lift not your hands to *It* for help – for it
As impotently rolls as you or I.

RUTHLESS RHYMES

Ruthless rhymes were made popular by Harry Graham in his book of the same name. They are rhymes where somebody usually meets a gruesome end but the verse is written in a jaunty and light manner. Thus the subject matter and the verse create an incongruity which makes them amusing. Ruthless rhymes belong in the area of **light verse**.

(see **Little Willie**)

*SAPPHIC VERSE

Sapphics are called after the Greek lyric poetess, Sappho and are one of the best known classical verse forms. Many English poets have written Sapphic verse in spite of the fact that it is based on two feet, the **dactyl** and the **trochee**, which are not as natural for English rhythms as the **iamb**.

The Form

- The **stanza** form is a **quatrain** (four lines).

- The first three lines are written in trochaic **pentameter** (five feet), except for the third foot of each line which is a dactyl.

- Thus the rhythm of each line is as follows: dum-di / dum-di / dum-di-di / dum-di / dum-di.

- The fourth line of each stanza has only two feet – a dactyl and a trochee; thus the rhythm is: dum-di-di / dum-di.

- There is no limit to the number of quatrains used for a poem.

- Rhyme is not used in this form.

Example:

From *Sapphics* by A. C. Swinburne

```
 ╱ ◡ | ╱    ◡ | ╱   ◡ ◡|╱  ◡ |╱  ◡
```
All the night sleep came not upon my eyelids,
Shed not I dew, nor I shook nor un|closed a I feather,
Yet with I lips shut I close and with I eyes of I iron
    Stood and be I held me.

SATIRE

SATIRE Satirical verse is poetry which attacks and ridicules, often employing a biting wit (see also **parody**). Its subjects will vary from general society and its mores, to vices of individual people, and even to institutions and ideas. Anything is 'fair game' for the satirist and satire is a form of protest, usually quite vehement in tone. Originally there was an element of moral correction involved and, to a certain extent, this is still the case with modern day satire.

The great English satirists have mainly written in prose (e.g. Jonathan Swift, Henry Fielding, Samuel Butler and George Orwell). However, notable verse satirists have been John Dryden, Alexander Pope and, particularly, Byron in his long poem, *Don Juan* (see **ottava rima**).

SEPTET

SEPTET A septet is a **stanza**, or whole poem, of seven lines, which may be written in any metre and with any rhyme scheme. The most common septet stanza form is **rhyme royal**.

SESTET
A sestet is a stanza, or whole poem, of six lines which can be written in any metre and with any rhyme scheme. It is also known as a sexain, **sextain** or sixain. The term, sestet, is also specifically applied to the second part of a **Petrarchan sonnet**.

*SESTINA
The sestina is an old medieval French form which has a system of repeated words. It was invented by the thirteenth century Provençal poet, Arnaut Daniel, and was used by both Dante and Petrarch in Italy. It is a complicated form but has proved an interesting challenge for English writers, many of whom have experimented with it, including the Elizabethan, Sir Philip Sidney, the nineteenth century poet, Swinburne, and W. H. Auden in the twentieth century.

The Form

- There are six **stanza**s of six lines each, followed by an **envoi** of three lines.

- The last words of each line occur in each stanza in a set order, as follows:

first stanza:	1, 2, 3, 4, 5, 6;
second stanza:	6, 1, 5, 2, 4, 3;
third stanza:	3, 6, 4, 1, 2, 5;
fourth stanza:	5, 3, 2, 6, 1, 4;
fifth stanza:	4, 5, 1, 3, 6, 2;
sixth stanza:	2, 4, 6, 5, 3, 1.

- The envoi contains all six words, two to a line, as follows:

first line:	2 (in the middle) and 5 (at the end);
second line:	4 (in the middle) and 3 (at the end);
third line:	6 (in the middle) and 1 (at the end).

- Sometimes the envoi contains only three of the words: (5, 3 and 1 in that order) at the ends of lines.

- Sometimes the order of the six words in the envoi may vary, as in the example below.

- Each line is usually written in **iamb**ic **pentameter** (although there may be occasional variations in rhythm as is common in this metre). The example below is in **tetrameter**.

Example:

Have a Good Time by W. H. Auden

'We have brought you,' they said, 'a map of the country;
Here is the line that runs to the vats,
This patch of green on the left is the wood,
We've pencilled an arrow to point out the bay.
No thank you, no tea; why look at the clock.
Keep it? Of course. It goes with our love.

We shall watch your future and send our love.
We lived for years, you know, in the country.
Remember at week-ends to wind up the clock.
We've wired to our manager at the vats.
The tides are perfectly safe in the bay,
But whatever you do don't go to the wood.

There's a flying trickster in that wood,
And we shan't be there to help with our love.
Keep fit by bathing in the bay,
You'll never catch fever then in the country.
You're sure of a settled job at the vats
If you keep their hours and live by the clock.'

He arrived at last; it was time by the clock.
He crossed himself as he passed the wood;
Black against evening sky the vats
Brought tears to his eyes as he thought of their love;
Looking out over the darkening country,
He saw the pier in the little bay.

At the week-ends the divers in the bay
Distracted his eyes from the bandstand clock;
When down with fever and in the country
A skein of swans above the wood
Caused him no terror; he came to love
The moss that grew on the derelict vats.

And he has met sketching at the vats
Guests from the new hotel in the bay;
Now, curious, following his love,
His pulses differing from the clock,
Finds consummation in the wood
And sees for the first time the country.

Sees water in the wood and trees by the bay,
Hears a clock striking near the vats;
'This is your country and the hour of love'.

The Rhymed Sestina

English writers have also experimented with rhyming sestinas, notably Swinburne. The pattern of repeated words needs to be different in order to avoid having rhyming **couplet**s in some of the stanzas. The form is in every other way the same as above.

● The pattern of repeated end-rhymes in the example below is as follows:

first stanza: 1, 2, 3, 4, 5, 6;
second stanza: 6, 1, 4, 3, 2, 5;
third stanza: 5, 6, 1, 4, 3, 2;
fourth stanza: 2, 5, 6, 1, 4, 3;
fifth stanza: 3, 2, 1, 6, 5, 4
sixth stanza: 4, 3, 2, 5, 6, 1.

● The pattern of the envoi is as follows:
1 and 4;
2 and 3;
5 and 6.

Example:

Sestina by A. C. Swinburne

I saw my soul at rest upon a day
As a bird sleeping in the nest of night,
Among soft leaves that give the starlight way
To touch its wings but not its eyes with light;
So that it knew as one in visions may,
And knew not as men waking, of delight.

This was the measure of my soul's delight;
It had no power of joy to fly by day,
Nor part in the large lordship of the light;
But in a secret moon-beholden way
Had all its will of dreams and pleasant night,
And all the love and life that sleepers may.

But such life's triumph as men waking may
It might not have to feed its faint delight
Between the stars by night and sun by day,
Shut up with green leaves and a little light;
Because its way was as a lost star's way,

A world's not wholly known of day or night.

All loves and dreams and sounds and gleams of night
Made it all music that such minstrels may,
And all they had they gave it of delight;
But in the full face of the fire of day
What place shall be for any starry light,
What part of heaven in all the wide sun's way?

Yet the soul woke not, sleeping by the way,
Watched as a nursling of the large-eyed night,
And sought no strength or knowledge of the day,
Nor closer touch conclusive of delight,
Nor mightier joy nor truer than dreamers may,
Nor more of song than they, nor more of light.

For who sleeps once and sees the secret light
Whereby sleep shows the soul a fairer way
Between the rise and rest of day and night,
Shall care no more to fare as all men may,
But be his place of pain or of delight,
There shall he dwell, beholding night as day.

Song, have thy day and take thy fill of light
Before the night be fallen across the way;
Sing while he may, man hath no long delight.

SEXTAIN (see sestet)

*SICILIAN OCTAVE The Sicilian octave is an Italian form of
stanza from the thirteenth century. It is related to ottava rima but
has hardly been used in English verse.

The Form

- There are eight lines of 11 syllables each, on a metrical pattern
  containing five or six strong stresses.

- The rhyme scheme is as follows: a, b, a, b, a, b, a, b.

- The stanza can be used on its own as a small poem, or in a series
  for longer poems.

SIMILE

A simile is a figure of speech related to **metaphor**. Similes compare two different things by uncovering a similarity between them. A simile uses one of two words to compare the two things, either *as* or *like* and these act as 'bridge' words. Some well-known examples are: 'as old as the hills', 'a face like thunder', 'a mind like a sieve', 'as wet as a fish' and 'as cunning as a fox'. When used in poetry, similes are more likely to employ the 'bridge' word *like* rather than *as*. Similes, along with metaphors, are important in poetry for creating colourful and memorable images.

Example:

1. From *Liberty* by Edward Thomas

The last light has gone out of the world, except
This moonlight lying on the ground like frost
Beyond the brink of the tall elm's shadow.

2. From *A Birthday* by Christina Rossetti

My heart is like a singing bird
Whose nest is in a watered shoot;
My heart is like an apple tree
Whose boughs are bent with thickset fruit;
My heart is like a rainbow shell
That paddles in a halcyon sea;
My heart is gladder than all these
Because my love is come to me.

*SONNET

The sonnet is a lyric poem with 14 lines and a strict rhyme scheme. It originated in Sicily in the thirteenth century and takes its name from an Italian word, *sonetto*, meaning 'little song'. There are four basic models of sonnets – the Petrarchan, the Shakespearean (or English), the Miltonic and the Spenserian, all named after the poets who either developed them or made them most popular. Sonnets were usually love poems to, or about, a favoured lady but they might also treat religious subjects. In most of the variations, the discussion of the theme over the fourteen lines splits naturally into an **octave** (eight lines) followed by a **sestet** (six lines).

A Midsummer Night's Dream, Act 3, Scene 1, by Shakespeare

Quince: 'Well, we will have such a prologue; and it shall be written in eight and six.'

The sonnet was introduced into English by Sir Thomas Wyatt in the early sixteenth century and soon became a very popular form amongst Elizabethan poets, such as Shakespeare, Spenser, and Sir Philip Sidney. Apart from the sonnets of John Milton in the seventeenth century, the form dropped out of fashion in England until the nineteenth century when it enjoyed a great revival. The Romantic poets, Wordsworth, Shelley and Keats, all wrote wonderful and memorable sonnets, as did later Victorians such as Elizabeth Barrett Browning and Gerard Manley Hopkins. English poets have continued to experiment with the sonnet, both with its form and range of subject matter. As a general rule modern experiments with sonnets adhere to only one aspect of the original – the 14 lines (and even that is not always the case). Rhyme schemes, line-lengths and metre may have no consistent pattern, or may not exist at all. It is sometimes difficult to see any connection with the original sonnet form which gave birth to such variations. However, once a writer has mastered any form, it is only by experimentation with it that new boundaries for prosody are created. After all, if Shakespeare and Spenser had not adapted the Petrarchan sonnet we might never have had some of the greatest poetry in the English canon.

The Forms

The Petrarchan Sonnet

- It has 14 lines, divided into two parts; the **octave** (eight lines) and the **sestet** (six lines).

- The octave introduces the theme of the poem, often presenting a longing, a doubt or a problem, and the sestet resolves it.

- Lines are written in **iamb**ic **pentameter** (di-dum, di-dum, di-dum, di-dum, di-dum) although subtle variations will occur as long as the five **foot** line is retained.

- There are only five rhyming sounds used at the ends of lines, and the rhyme scheme is as follows: a, b, b, a, a, b, b, a, c, d, e, c, d, e.

- The sestet may also rhyme c, d, c, d, c, d, thus creating a sonnet of only four rhyming sounds.

Example:

> ### *Upon Westminster Bridge Sept. 3 1802* by William Wordsworth
>
> | | |
> |---|---|
> | Earth has not anything to show more fair: | a |
> | Dull would he be of soul who could pass by | b |
> | A sight so touching in its majesty: | b |
> | This City now doth, like a garment, wear | a |
> | The beauty of the morning; silent, bare, | a |
> | Ships, towers, domes, theatres, and temples lie | b |
> | Open unto the fields, and to the sky; | b |
> | All bright and glittering in the smokeless air. | a |
> | Never did sun more beautifully steep | c |
> | In his first splendour, valley, rock, or hill; | d |
> | Ne'er saw I, never felt, a calm so deep! | c |
> | The river glideth at his own sweet will: | d |
> | Dear God! the very houses seem asleep; | c |
> | And all that mighty heart is lying still! | d |

The Shakespearean Sonnet (also called the English Sonnet)

● It has 14 lines written in **iambic pentameter** with subtle variations of **rhythm** as long as the five **foot** line is retained.

● A natural break in meaning usually occurs between the first eight lines (the **octave**) and the next six lines (the **sestet**).

● Other smaller shifts in meaning occur after every four lines (each **quatrain**) and the poem finishes with a rhyming **couplet**.

● The rhyme scheme is as follows: a, b, a, b, c, d, c, d, e, f, e, f, g, g.

Example:

> ### *Sonnet 12* by William Shakespeare
>
> | | |
> |---|---|
> | When I do count the clock that tells the time, | a |
> | And see the brave day sunk in hideous night; | b |
> | When I behold the violet past prime, | a |
> | And sable curls all silver'd o'er with white; | b |
> | When lofty trees I see barren of leaves, | c |
> | Which erst from heat did canopy the herd, | d |
> | And summer's green all girded up in sheaves | c |
> | Borne on the bier with white and bristly beard; | d |

Then of thy beauty do I question make   e
That thou among the wastes of time must go,   f
Since sweets and beauties do themselves forsake,   e
And die as fast as they see others grow;   f
And nothing 'gainst Time's scythe can make defence   g
Save breed, to brave him when he takes thee hence.   g
(erst = once)

The Spenserian Sonnet

- It has 14 lines written in **iambic pentameter** with subtle variations of rhythm as long as the five **foot** line is retained.

- It has an interlocking rhyme scheme. Spenser enjoyed such rhyme schemes but few poets since then have been drawn to this sonnet form (see also **Spenserian stanza**).

- The rhyme scheme is as follows: a, b, a, b, b, c, b, c, c, d, c, d, e, e.

Example:

Easter by Edmund Spenser

Most glorious Lord of lyfe, that on this day,   a
Didst make thy triumph over death and sin: b
And having harrow'd hell, didst bring away   a
Captivity thence captive us to win: b
This joyous day, deare Lord, with joy begin,   b
And grant that we, for whom thou diddest dye,   c
Being with thy deare blood clene washt from sin,   b
May live for ever in felicity.   c
And that thy love we weighing worthily,   c
May likewise love thee for the same againe: d
And for thy sake that all lyke deare didst buy,   c
With love may one another entertayne.   d
So let us love, deare love, lyke as we ought,   e
Love is the lesson which the Lord us taught.   e

The Miltonic Sonnet

- The only difference between this kind of sonnet and the Petrarchan sonnet is that there is no natural break, or turning point, in meaning between the octave and the sestet. The rhyme scheme is the same, although it may vary more in the sestet (see **Petrarchan Sonnet**, above for full details of the form.)

Example:

On His Blindness by John Milton

When I consider how my light is spent,	a
Ere half my days, in this dark world and wide,	b
And that one talent which is death to hide	b
Lodged with me useless, though my soul more bent	a
To serve therewith my Maker, and present	a
My true account, lest he returning chide,	b
'Doth God exact day-labour, light denied?'	b
I fondly ask. But Patience, to prevent	a
That murmur, soon replies: 'God doth not need	c
Either man's work or his own gifts; who best	d
Bear his mild yoke, they serve him best. His state	e
Is kingly: thousands at his bidding speed,	c
And post o'er land and ocean without rest;	d
They also serve who only stand and wait.'	e

Variations on the Sonnet

There have been so many different variations – in metre, rhyme and progress of meaning – suffice it to say that the form is open to experimentation. The following are just two examples where the changes can be said to have worked magnificently.

1. *Ozymandias* by Percy Bysshe Shelley

I met a traveller from an antique land	a
Who said: Two vast and trunkless legs of stone	b
Stand in the desert . . . . Near them, on the sand,	a
Half sunk, a shattered visage lies, whose frown,	b
And wrinkled lip, and sneer of cold command,	a
Tell that its sculptor well those passions read	c
Which yet survive, stamped on these lifeless things,	d
The hand that mocked them, and the heart that fed:	c
And on the pedestal these words appear:	e
'My name is Ozymandias, king of kings:	d

Look on my works, ye Mighty, and despair!'	e
Nothing beside remains. Round the decay	f
Of that colossal wreck, boundless and bare	e
The lone and level sands stretch far away.	f

In the second example, the rhyme scheme is that of the standard
Petrarchan sonnet but the metre is very different (see **sprung
rhythm**).

2. *The Windhover* by Gerard Manley Hopkins
To Christ our Lord

I caught this morning morning's minion, king-
dom of daylight's dauphin, dapple-dawn-drawn Falcon, in his
   riding
Of the rolling level underneath him steady air, and striding
High there, how he rung upon the rein of a wimpling wing
In his ecstasy! then off, off forth on swing,
As a skate's heel sweeps smooth on a bow-bend: the hurl and
   gliding
Rebuffed the big wind. My heart in hiding
Stirred for a bird, – the achieve of, the mastery of the thing!

Brute beauty and valour and act, oh, air, pride, plume, here
Buckle! AND the fire that breaks from thee then, a billion
Times told lovelier, more dangerous, O my chevalier!

No wonder of it: shéer plód makes plough down sillion
Shine, and blue-bleak embers, ah my dear,
Fall, gall themselves, and gash gold-vermilion.

*SPENSERIAN STANZA Spenser invented this stanza form
for his long poem, *The Faerie Queene*, in the late sixteenth century. It
is similar to his version of the sonnet, with its linked rhyme scheme,
but has only nine lines. The form was not much used again until
the eighteenth century, but it was the nineteenth century Romantic
poets, Byron, Keats and Shelley, who really explored its full potential
in their work. Some of the best examples can be found in Byron's
Childe Harold's Pilgrimage, Shelley's *Adonais*, and Keats' *Eve of St
Agnes*.

The Form

- It has nine lines – eight are in **iambic pentameter**, and the ninth is written in iambic **hexameter** (an **alexandrine**).

- The rhyme scheme is as follows: a, b, a, b, b, c, b, c, c.

Example:

From *Eve of St Agnes* by John Keats

Which was, to lead him, in close secrecy,	a
Even to Madeline's chamber, and there hide	b
Him in a closet, of such privacy	a
That he might see her beauty unespied,	b
And win perhaps that night a peerless bride,	b
While legion'd fairies paced the coverlet,	c
And pale enchantment held her sleepy-eyed.	b
Never on such a night have lovers met,	c
Since Merlin paid his Demon all the monstrous debt.	c

STANZA A stanza is a group of lines making up what is commonly referred to as a verse (although, strictly speaking, verse is either the general term for poetry, or it is one line of poetry). There are many different patterns of stanza, according to the length and metre of lines, the number of lines, and the rhyme scheme. The most common length of stanza in English verse is four lines or a **quatrain** (see also **couplet, tercet, quintain, sestet, septet,** and **octave**).

(see starred entries (*) for fixed forms for a range of possible stanza patterns)

*TANKA Tanka is a Japanese short lyric form written to a pattern of syllables without regular metre and rhyme (see also **haiku, naga-uta** and **renga**). It is considered to be the classic Japanese verse form. It has not been as popular as haiku among western writers but there has been some interest in the form more recently.

The Form

- It has five lines containing 31 syllables: five in the first line, seven in the second, five in the third, seven in the fourth, seven in the fifth (5,7,5,7,7).

- There is no rhyme and no regular metre.

Example:

Rain sets in again,
Wetting the spider hanging
From the window ledge.
O weave your web against this
Inevitable autumn.

SB

TERCET A tercet is a stanza of three lines linked by rhyme, notably in the forms **terza rima** and **villanelle**. It may also be applied to the two three-line parts of the sestet in a sonnet. It is often interchangeable as a term with **triplet**.

*TERZA RIMA Terza rima is a series of three-line stanzas (**tercet**s) which have a pattern of chain rhyming. It was the form used by Dante in his long poem, *The Divine Comedy*, and was introduced into English verse in the sixteenth century by Sir Thomas Wyatt. It has not proved a very popular verse form with English poets, although there are examples by Byron, Browning and, most famously, Shelley in his *Ode to the West Wind*.

The Form

● Each stanza has three lines – usually in **iamb**ic **pentameter** in English verse. There is an extra line (or a couplet) at the end, rhyming with the middle line of the last tercet.

● The rhyme scheme is as follows: a, b, a   b, c, b   c, d, c   d, e, d   e, f, e etc.

Example:

From *Ode to the West Wind* by Percy Bysshe Shelley

O wild West Wind, thou breath of Autumn's being,	a
Thou from whose unseen presence the leaves dead	b
Are driven like ghosts from an enchanter fleeing,	a
Yellow, and black, and pale, and hectic red,	b
Pestilence-stricken multitudes! O thou	c
Who chariotest to their dark wintry bed	b

The wingéd seeds, where they lie cold and low,	c
Each like a corpse within its grave, until	d
Thine azure sister of the Spring shall blow	c
Her clarion o'er the dreaming earth, and fill	d
(Driving sweet buds like flocks to feed in air)	e
With living hues and odours plain and hill;	d
Wild Spirit, which art moving everywhere;	e
Destroyer and preserver; hear, O hear!	e

*TRIOLET The triolet was originally a French form of verse which has repeated lines and only two rhymes. It has not been a popular form for English poets although writers such as Austin Dobson and W. E. Henley experimented with it in the nineteenth century to some effect. However, in more recent times some poets, notably Gavin Ewart and Wendy Cope, have enjoyed using the triolet for humorous verse for which it appears very suited. The examples below show the form both in humorous and more serious vein.

The Form

● It has eight lines and only two rhyming sounds.

● The first line is repeated as lines 4 and 7 and the second line is repeated as line 8. The punctuation may be changed so that although the words are repeated the sense may be slightly altered.

● The rhyme scheme is as follows (repeated lines have capital letters): **A**, **B**, a, **A**, a, b, **A**, **B**.

● A regular metre and line-length is used for each line, but this can be whatever the writer wishes e.g. **dimeter, trimeter, tetrameter** or **pentameter** etc.

Examples:

1. *Urceus Exit* by Austin Dobson

I intended an Ode,	**A**
And it turn'd to a Sonnet;	**B**
It began *à la mode*,	a

I intended an Ode;	**A**
But Rose cross'd the road	a
In her latest new bonnet;	b
I intended an Ode;	**A**
And it turn'd to a Sonnet.	**B**

2. *Triolet* by Robert Bridges

When first we met, we did not guess
That Love would prove so hard a master;
Of more than common friendliness
When first we met we did not guess
Who could foretell the sore distress,
The inevitable disaster,
When first we met? We did not guess
That Love would prove so hard a master.

TRIPLET
A triplet is a three-line stanza (see also **tercet**).

The term may also be applied to three lines of verse occurring within a poem. When this happens the triplet follows a different verse pattern from the rest of the poem.

A triplet is most often three lines with the same end-rhyming sounds.

It is also the term applied to three successive rhyming lines in a poem which is otherwise written in couplets.

The following poem is written in **heroic couplet**s but ends with two triplets.

Example:

From *The Coronation* by Thomas Hardy

'If I were up there where the parsons sit,
In one of my gold robes, I'd see to it!'

'But you are not,' Charles chuckled. 'You are here,
And never will know the sun again, my dear!'

'Yea,' whispered those whom no one had addressed;
'With slow, sad march, amid a folk distressed,
We were brought here to take our dusty rest.

'And here, alas, in darkness laid below,'
We'll wait and listen, and endure the show. . . .
Clamour dogs kingship; afterwards not so!'

*VILLANELLE

The villanelle is a French form with a strict rhyme and metric pattern which uses repeated lines as **refrains**. It was originally a poem for pastoral subjects and the form as we now know it was probably fixed in the sixteenth century. A few English writers experimented with it in the nineteenth century, but it became more popular in the twentieth century when poets, such as W. H. Auden, Dylan Thomas, and William Empson, moved away from the pastoral theme and wrote some memorable villanelles on more serious subjects. Perhaps the most well-known of these are Empson's *Missing Dates* ('Slowly the poison the whole blood stream fills . . .'), Auden's *If I could Tell You* ('Time will say nothing but I told you so . . .'), and Dylan Thomas's *Do not Go Gentle into that Good Night*. Other poets, such as Gavin Ewart and Wendy Cope, have found the villanelle ideally suited to light verse and the form has enjoyed something of a renaissance in recent times.

The Form

● There are five **tercets** followed by a **quatrain** – six **stanza**s in all.

● Theoretically, a villanelle may have any odd number of tercets from three upwards, although in practice, most poets tend to use five.

● Lines are usually written in **iamb**ic **pentameter** (di-dum, di-dum, di-dum, di-dum, di-dum), although earlier Victorian villanelles tended to be in iambic **tetrameter**.

● Only two rhyming sounds are used throughout the poem.

● The first and third lines (of the first tercet) are repeated at set intervals, and come together as a rhyming **couplet** at the end of the quatrain.

● The rhyme scheme is as follows (the repeated lines are shown as A^1 and A^2):
A^1, b, A^2 a, b, A^1 a, b, A^2 a, b, A^1 a, b, A^2 a, b, A^1, A^2.

The poem on the following page is in iambic tetrameter.

Example:

Villanelle by W. E. Henley

A dainty thing's the Villanelle	**A¹**
Sly, musical, a jewel in rhyme,	b
It serves its purpose passing well.	**A²**
A double-clappered silver bell	a
That must be made to clink in chime,	b
A dainty thing's the Villanelle;	**A¹**
And if you wish to flute a spell,	a
Or ask a meeting 'neath the lime,	b
It serves its purpose passing well.	**A²**
You must not ask of it the swell	a
Of organs grandiose and sublime –	b
A dainty thing's the Villanelle;	**A¹**
And, filled with sweetness, as a shell	a
Is filled with sound, and launched in time,	b
It serves its purpose passing well.	**A²**
Still fair to see and good to smell	a
As in the quaintness of its prime,	b
A dainty thing's the Villanelle,	**A¹**
It serves its purpose passing well.	**A²**

Further Reading

1. John Whitworth, *Writing Poetry*, A & C Black, 2001.

2. Frances Stillman, *The Poet's Manual and Rhyming Dictionary*, Thames & Hudson, 1966.

3. Vernon Scannell, *How to Enjoy Poetry*, Piatkus, 1983.

4. Michael Baldwin, *The Way to Write Poetry*, Elmtree, 1982.

5. Ted Hughes, *Poetry in the Making*, Faber and Faber, 1969.

6. John Hollander, *Rhyme's Reason*, Yale University Press, (enlarged and new edition), 1989.

7. G. S. Fraser, *Metre, Rhyme and Free Verse*, Methuen, 1970.

8. Philip Hobsbaum, *Metre, Rhythm and Verse Form*, Routledge, 1996.

9. J. A. Cuddon, *A Dictionary of Literary Terms*, Penguin, 1976.

10. Karl Beckson and Arthur Ganz, *Literary Terms*, Farrar, Straus and Giroux, 1960.